MW00777245

THE COMPLETE GUIDE TO
CLIMBING
(BY BIKE)
IN THE SOUTHEAST

*A guide to cycling climbing and the most difficult
hill climbs in the Southeast United States*

John Summerson

Extreme Press
405 Kettle Court
Winston-Salem, NC 27104
336 659-7600
Extreme.press@yahoo.com

First Edition, May 2009

Copyright © 2009 John Summerson

All photos by the author unless otherwise noted

Library of Congress Catalog Card Number 2009900212

ISBN 13: 978-0-9792571-1-7

"The best climbers do not suffer less; they just suffer faster" Chris Boardman

Front cover - Tour of Georgia riders on Brasstown Bald - photo by Bryan McKenney

Back cover - Cherohala Skyway in North Carolina; inset - Lookout Mountain in Georgia/Tennessee

Table of Contents

Alabama

Georgia

North Carolina

South Carolina

Tennessee

Virginia

West Virginia

Preface

The Blue Ridge and Appalachian Mountains in the Southeast United States are among the most beautiful in the World. With this topographic rise comes the creation of many challenging hill climbs. Its beauty well known, to a cyclist the topography is even more interesting as any location with multiple mountains is bound to have multiple ascents of interest. Having collected climb data from all over the United States while preparing the book 'The Complete Guide to Climbing By Bike'and with interest in climbing growing, I realized that many worthwhile climbs were being left out of the nationwide guide simply because they were not among the very most difficult. This was particularly evident in the Southeast U.S. which contains a large number of challenging ascents.

Having lived in the region for many years has allowed me the opportunity to ascend just about every worthwhile hill in the Southeast U.S. and while no one knows the local climbs better than those that live nearby, I think this database is comprehensive but likely not complete. At the least this data is now available in one place for those seeking this information. Today I still get a sense of satisfaction from finding another particularly challenging hill to climb so please send any other climbs worthy of mention to the author for future editions.

Introduction

Road bike cycling is one of the most popular sports in the world and the biggest challenge within the sport, and its most intriguing aspect, is hill climbing. Major professional cycling tours such as the Tour de France are usually won and lost in the mountains. But why climb the hill? Climbing is also the most difficult part of cycling, requiring great energy and effort and on tough hills or going all out, producing pain. Why, then, do cyclists routinely engage in a painful activity that can result, as they themselves describe, in great suffering for the sole purpose of reaching the top? In the case of professional riders it could be argued that they are paid to do it. For others answers may include losing weight, improving one's racing ability or fitness level, or getting back to where you started. But I think the real answer is because it's there. This simple phrase sums up the main reason people undertake physical challenges. Be it mountain climbing, distance running or peak-bagging by bike, the main reason cyclists will tolerate the pain is for the physical and mental challenge itself. Hills are there to be beaten.

For years, major cycling events such as the Tour de France have evoked the image of the lone rider struggling up sheer alpine pitches, straining their physical limits. Cycling greats such as Eddy Merckx, Bernard Hinault and Lance Armstrong, while very complete all-around riders, became legends in the sport in large part from their climbing exploits. The mountains add an almost mythic quality to races as the riders are seen overcoming obstacles that extend beyond the actual asphalt, rock and dirt upon which they climb. Even average cyclists feel the allure of attempting difficult climbs and achieve tremendous satisfaction from a successful summit. It sounds pretty simple. Find a mountain with a paved road to the top and then pedal up it. However, hill climbing is not easy, as certain climbs involve ascents of thousands of vertical feet. Elite riders can race to the top but success for most involves just getting there.

As the Southeast United States has many challenging hills to conquer, this book is meant to be a resource for road bike hill climbing and to describe the most difficult climbs in the area. Other ascents are included for reasons such as a steep grade or some other unique aspects.

Georgia's Wolfpen Gap

Climbing

No one may know when the first significant hill was climbed on a bicycle but the first documentation of major ascents occurred in stage races which originated in Europe, the oldest being the Tour de France. It is interesting to note that the first two Tours (first held in 1903) did not include any mountain passes. Bikes were heavy, single speed (and brake) behemoths while many roads were unpaved. Some felt that the riders of the day could not complete big climbs and that adding them to the race route would ruin the Tour. It was not until 1905 that significant climbs were added, the very first being the Ballon d'Alsace in the Vosges Mountains. In 1910 the first major, high altitude passes were added (four major climbs in the Pyrenees Mountains including the now famous Tourmalet) which resulted in a great deal of criticism directed at race organizers that the routes were too difficult. As is often the case human potential was underestimated as many riders of that era conquered the climbs in dramatic fashion. In contrast, 1910 was also the year that the broom wagon was introduced to sweep riders up who could not finish the stage. In 1911 the first major climb in the Alps was added (Col de Galibier) with spectacular results. Instead of being a detriment, the uphill duels captured the public imagination and added to the popularity of the event. The race route every year thereafter has contained many significant climbs. Other major tours that followed also began to include hills along their routes. In 1933 the Tour de France and the Giro d'Italia (Italy's national tour) began recognizing the best climbers in the field (Spain's Vicente Trueba was the first winner in the Tour along with Alfredo Binda in the Giro). Most of the major stage races now recognize this accomplishment as the cyclists earn points based upon their finish in a climb and its difficulty. The cyclist with the most accumulated points is awarded the Polka Dot Jersey as the winner of the king of the mountains competition.

The performances of great early climbers such as Alfredo Binda, Fausto Coppi and Charley Gaul continued to increase the popularity of the major tours. These events made climbs such as the Tourmalet and L'Alpe d'Huez in France and Stelvio in Italy as well known to cycling fans as the Daytona Speedway or Yankee Stadium are to U.S. racing and baseball fans respectively. The mountains allowed bike races to become truly great as the event rose beyond the personal concerns of the cyclists to reflect life as a whole. Today hill climbing is more popular than ever and within multi-stage races those with hilltop finishes are usually the most anticipated and best attended stages of the race. Racing fans know that hills offer the best opportunity to view the drama within the peloton as it struggles through the most difficult and important element in any race. Climbing adds the mythic quality of overcoming obstacles that continues to be associated with the major cycling tours and which has produced many memorable moments. Ascending difficult hills is about struggle and perseverance and it is these aspects that have made conquering the mountains the heart and soul of cycling.

About This Guidebook

Road bike cycling and hill climbing in particular are enjoying a surge in popularity in the U.S., perhaps due to the success of the major road bike races and Lance Armstrong and/or the ongoing fitness/physical challenge craze in this country. In spite of growing popularity however, there is little published information on the location of area road bike hill climbs and very little accurate data on the length and elevation gain of these climbs. Many roads are hilly but that is not the intent of this guide. The location, description and profiling of major individual hills in the Southeast U.S. is its aim. As such, I set out to publish a guide for those cyclists looking for this information and to collect data for climb comparison purposes. You will have many of these hills all to yourself as the majority are not well known.

In addition to listing the location of climbs I wanted to provide accurate data on their length, grade, elevation gain and other statistics. While there are various data available it is important when compiling data to reduce the variability of measurement that can occur from multiple sources and to apply consistent definitions to hill climbs. The listed statistics for climbs often vary as different people use different starting and ending points and less than accurate measurement procedures. At times climb gradients are reported inaccurately or overestimated such as when the maximum grade is sometimes considered the average grade. In addition, climbs are sometimes profiled by using mapping software to analyze roads that have been superimposed upon a topographic map. Roads are at times not accurately laid down within map contours which can result in less than accurate measurements. The measurements in this guide were all obtained directly on each climb and compiled by one source. That said, truly precise data is hard to come by and errors in measurement and recording are bound to happen.

There are hundreds of climbs in and around the mountains of the Southeast so obviously they all cannot be included in these pages. What this guidebook does include are the most difficult road bike climbs in the area that are open for bikes (see appendices for rankings). Other climbs are described due to a steep grade, or other unique aspect such as outstanding scenery (along with significant climbing), cycling history or some combination of the above. Appendices in this guide rank climbs by overall difficulty, average grade, elevation gain and several other categories. The author has first hand knowledge of 135 out of the 140 (96%) described climbs in this guide. Climbs with estimated statistics are noted. It is a difficult task to attempt to record and document all of the significant climbs within the Southeast so if noteworthy ascents were left out please send the appropriate information to the author.

While some of the ascents in this guide are for the serious road cyclist only, there are many moderate climbs for the rider looking to improve their climbing skills and/or fitness level. Be sure to know your fitness and ability level before you tackle the longer and/or more difficult hills in this book. Start with the shorter, less steep climbs and progress from there. As all are located in the mountains, the scenery along the way is usually spectacular and will help ease the pain of a tough ascent.

Defining A Hill Climb

Along with the location and statistics of Southeast U.S. climbs, this guide will attempt to standardize the definition of a hill climb. That is, what constitutes a climb, what are the starting and ending points and, if multiple approaches, the shortest route to the top. The start and finish of most climbs are generally easy to define as they have definite beginnings and endings. Others are a bit vague, particularly along shallow-grade stretches of road. The starting point of these types of climbs is considered to be the transition from flat to a definite climb or a significant change in elevation for very gently climbing stretches of roads. A good example of the latter is the north side of Red Mountain Pass in Colorado along Route 550 (one of the most spectacular climbs in the U.S.). Route 550 actually begins to climb many miles to the north of its listed start in Ouray, CO. However, the grade is so slight that the author believes this should not be considered a hill climb. Once in Ouray it is quite clear where the true hill begins as there is a significant change in grade right in the middle of town.

Another topic worthy of discussion regarding climb definitions is a clarification of their ending points. Most climbs have an easy-to-define end such as Mount Mitchell in North Carolina which dead-ends very close to the top of the mountain. However, some do not. For climbs that do not dead end, the top is considered when the road descends from that point (such as mountain passes), or if it reaches a significant flat without significant climbing beyond it. A good example of the latter is Brayton Mountain Road in TN. At its listed top the road flattens out. Over the next few miles the road rolls up and down before peaking at an altitude that is slightly higher than the listed climb

Scenic Cherohala Skyway in NC

The north side of Roan Mountain in TN

17

peak. However, the additional climbing is not constant and is over such shallow grade that the additional riding does not constitute climbing in the author's mind.

Another issue in defining climbs is how flat sections and/or descents along the route factor in. A climb can have small flats and/or infrequent small descents and still be considered a continuous ascent as long as the vast majority of the route is uphill (< 10% of the route is flats/descents). Many major hill climbs have small descents along the way but these sections always lead to significant additional climbing. Some very good rides with serious elevation gain however contain multiple flats/descents and are not included. These would include Route 130 in South Carolina; a very entertaining ride that climbs a significant distance but that has too much of its route along flat and/or descending terrain.

Some climbs may have a single major flat/descent (no more than one mile in length) if there is extended, significant climbing both before and after the flat/descent. For example, Mount Mitchell in North Carolina has a single major descent along its route but because there is significant climbing both before and after the descent it is considered a single climb. If a climb has more than one major flat/descent along its route it is considered two separate climbs. For instance, route 168 from Fresno to Kaiser Pass in California has more than 8000 feet of elevation gain along its route but there are several major descents along the way so the route is actually several different climbs. Mount Hamilton near San Jose, California is another example; it contains three uphill sections between two fairly major descents and while the climbing sections are worthy in themselves, the route from bottom to top is not considered by most to be one hill climb.

Definitions of Terms

This guide will use several terms to describe each climb which are defined below:

Total elevation - This is the elevation gained in feet from the starting point to the top of the climb. If a climb has descents within it this additional climbing is not included in the total elevation gained. Elevations were measured using global positioning satellite (GPS) positions from which a very accurate elevation was then determined by plotting the fixed point using a topographic software program.

Length - This is the distance of the climb in miles. If you are retracing your route back to the starting point, in order to determine the total distance of the ride, simply double the climb's length. Climb lengths were measured by automobile odometer (at least two measures and averaged) and cycle computer.

Average Grade (maximum grade) - This is the average percent grade or steepness of the climb and is expressed as a percentage (8%). The grade assigned to each hill is the average grade over the entire climb. The higher the percent grade, the steeper the climb. Percent grade is determined by dividing the elevation gain by the length of the climb. The maximum grade is just that. The measured maximum gradient must extend all the way across the road (a very steep inside corner that could be bypassed for instance does not qualify) and be at least twenty feet in length. Maximum gradient was measured by gradiometer. In the listed climb descriptions the distance and elevation data only reflect the contiguous portion of the road that is part of the climb. If the climb includes small flats or descents, they are included in the distance but do not contribute to the net elevation gain. Thus the average grade may not in some cases accurately represent the true nature of the climb. That is, there are usually sections on the climb that are steeper than the average grade along with sections that are less steep than the average grade.

Rating - There are several formulas available to rank climbs. All have shortcomings and have received criticism. In major races such as the Tour de France climbs are ranked using a numeric scale from 4 (easiest) to 1 with an extra classification describing the most difficult climbs as hors categoire or 'beyond category'. There are general guidelines for these categorizations that involve length and grade. However there are not precise definitions for each category and often the ratings are not applied consistently. In addition, climbs are often ranked according to their placement within a race stage meaning that a climb towards the end of a stage may be categorized as a 2 when the same climb may be a 3 (easier) if placed at the beginning of the stage. You may also have noticed that more recently certain climbs used in the Tour de France have been receiving a more difficult rating than for previous tours (call it hill inflation perhaps), regardless of their placement in a stage. The elevation reached within a climb is not taken into account in this and most other ratings systems as well. As increasing elevation has deleterious effects on physical performance, this factor should be taken into consideration. The point here is that a more accurate formula is needed and the one listed below is an attempt to more precisely quantify the difficulty of a climb and has taken into account the climb's elevation gain, average grade, altitude, surface and grade variability:

Square root of the average grade x total elevation gain x altitude adjustment (see altitude adjustment description) x grade variability (see grade variability adjustment description).

Altitude adjustment: Altitude research indicates that human performance shows a noticeable performance detriment beginning at approximately 2000 feet elevation of approximately 1% with subsequent performance deficits with increasing altitude and duration of activity. There are other elements that affect performance at altitude but vary by individual and at this point in time are very difficult if not impossible to quantify. The author acknowledges that the adjustment presented here is an estimation of the effects of altitude on performance.

Grade variability adjustment: If a climb has two or more segments where the grade of the segment exceeds the average climb grade by at least five percentage points the rating is adjusted by 0.025 (assumption that grade variability results in a slightly more difficult climb) for each of those sections. Very few climbs meet this criterion.

As you can see from the climb rankings there is very little difference in the numeric rating of many of the climbs. So little in fact that you will have a very difficult time discerning the differences while on the bike. All that having been said, there are too many variables involved to precisely rank a climb numerically and it is not the main intent of this guide to do so. While the author believes this rating system is an improvement over other models it is hoped that these ratings, while serving as a general guide to compare climbs, will also serve to spur debate and perhaps eventually a truly accurate rating system.

Directions - The starting point for almost all directions for climbs listed in this guidebook is the nearest town, some of which are very tiny places. A good road map will be helpful to locate and reach many of these locations. I would recommend the North American Road Atlas from AAA as it contains a town index for each state but any national/state highway road map will do.

Rules of the Road

• Wear a helmet.

• Follow the same driving rules as motorists and be sure to obey all traffic patterns and road signs.

• Wear bright colors so you are more visible to motorists.

• Ride single file on busy roads so that motorized vehicles can pass.

• Use hand signals to alert motorists to your next move.

• Ride with traffic and not against it.

• Make eye contact with drivers and assume they do not see you.

• Try to avoid riding in foggy, rainy or windy conditions.

- Be alert for sewer grates, manhole covers, cattle guards, oily pavement, gravel, wet leaves and ice.

- Give parked cars a wide berth.

- Many of these listed climbs are fairly long rides so go prepared with an extra tube along with pump, tool kit, rain gear, food and plenty of fluids at all times.

- It is usually best to ride with a partner or partners. In case of emergency one rider can go for help if needed.

Pre-Ride Check:

- Check the tires for proper inflation.

- Check the brakes for proper traction.

- Check all quick releases to make sure they are tight.

- Check the chain for tightness.

- Check all nuts and bolts.

- Spin your wheels through frame and brakes.

- Make sure you have all necessary gear for the particular climb/ride.

- Bring a positive attitude along whenever possible.

Improving Climbing Ability

For new cyclists, hill climbing is one of the most daunting aspects of riding. More experienced cyclists, however, enjoy climbing and regard tough hills as a challenge. It is a great feeling to make a solid climb and then enjoy the descent down the other side. The simplest way to improve your climbing technique and the best training for climbing is to climb; that is, to incorporate hills into your rides. However, don't start climbing big hills until you have built up an adequate cycling fitness base. Try to accumulate a significant amount of relatively flat riding first. At that point add shorter/moderate grade hills to your rides and work your way up to the longer and/or steeper climbs. Incorporating hills in your riding will not make them any shorter but eventually they will feel that way.

Cycling Techniques for Climbing

Improving your basic cycling techniques can also improve your climbing ability. It is important to maintain a smooth, steady rhythm as you pedal up the hill. Unless very short in length, start a climb with as slow a pace as possible. This will allow you to develop a rhythm which not only includes the pedaling cadence but breathing as well. Breathe slowly and deeply as this will help establish a smooth pedaling cadence. Obviously in your pedal stroke it is much easier to apply force to the pedals when your foot is on the down stroke. However, this results in uneven power output contributing to slight accelerations and decelerations of the bike which becomes exaggerated when climbing. To remedy this try to lift your knee and drag your foot backwards across the bottom of the pedal stroke, pulling upwards slightly on the upstroke and pulling the pedal forward across the top of its rotation.

There are several other factors to consider when climbing. First, make sure you have the right gears. At least a 39-tooth small chain ring in front and a 25-tooth rear gear (a 27 or 28 is even better if you will be riding consistently on steep hills). Upon encountering a hill, do not shift too soon as this can result in a momentum loss from a high RPM spinning effect. Conversely, you must not end up in a gear that is too large which tends to tire the rider out. The proper climbing cadence varies among individuals. The idea with gearing is to maintain a cadence that is comfortable, shifting as you tire and the RPM's start to drop. Basically, if the gradient varies on the climb adjust your gearing so that your cadence and level of effort are maximized.

Another factor is whether to sit or stand during the ascent. Seated is more energy efficient but a standing position can produce much more power. A simple rule to start with is that if the hill is long, climb in the saddle, and if short or while attacking, stand. Reality dictates that on most challenging hills you will do both. For most of the climb you will find it is more efficient to sit in the saddle. Put your hands on the top of the brake hoods or handlebars and keep them relaxed. Try to change their positioning periodically. The upper body should not be crunched forward too far and the shoulders should be open. This will allow for easier breathing as the climb continues. Relax your upper body as well, as this will decrease oxygen demands. Your weight should be over the cranks to maximize power during the pedal stroke. Try not to bounce on the pedals as you shift from side to side. Developing a rhythm that combines pedaling and breathing will make a big difference in your climbing efficiency. At times you will need to stand such as on very steep sections or when sprinting past a fellow rider. Just before you stand, shift to a higher gear as you can generate more power in this position (shift back when you sit down again). As you come off of the saddle continue with an even pedal stroke and push your hands forward. Come out of the saddle on the down stroke to minimize loss of momentum.

Specific Training for Hill Climbing

While the physiology of human performance training is much more understood today than in the past, training is still as much art as science. That is, there is more than one way to improve performance. However, perhaps the more important considerations are time and commitment. Time to train is obviously limited for most. With that in mind it is paramount that this limited time is put to good use. Intensity is the key with adequate rest for recovery. Particularly with hill climbing which involves very intense bursts of effort, adequate recovery is essential to avoid overtraining and burnout. In addition, train consistently for best results. Develop specific climbing goals and a plan to reach those goals. Listen to your body and back off if needed. Commit to climbing success and it will likely follow.

Good climbers have certain attributes that contribute to their success. All have an endurance base and have developed solid power to weight ratios which gives the ability to generate greater amounts of force with each pedal stroke. They also have high anaerobic endurance which results in greater levels of lactic acid tolerance. Training to improve climbing ability should focus on these physiologic aspects.

Build a Base

As previously mentioned make sure you have a solid cycling base before adding significant climbing to your riding and attempting the interval routines described later in this section. You should complete many miles of distance riding on mostly flat terrain to build your endurance base before moving on to more specialized routines that target climbing ability. The amount of time needed will vary by individual, ranging from several months to several years of regular road cycling depending on age, health and fitness level. After a period of mainly flat riding, add moderate hills to your regular endurance rides. As you progress, add longer and steeper hills.

Power to Weight Ratio

Climbing ability has a strong correlation with power to weight ratio; in fact it is perhaps the most accurate predictor of climbing success. As you may have noticed, the climbing specialists on the pro tour are almost all very lean (the late Marco Pantani comes to mind). Thus, climbing can be improved by increasing power, losing body weight or, for the greatest results, a combination of the two. Even a relatively small weight loss (3-5 lbs) can produce significant improvement. Much information is available regarding losing weight so this guide will not attempt to add to that body of knowledge. Just keep in mind that weight loss can lead to reductions in power output (to maintain power lose as much fat and as little muscle as possible). Increasing cycling power will be touched upon in the following sections and comes about through specific training.

Regarding the advantages of lower weight, do not forget your bike. As long as component stiffness is not compromised (stiffer rims and frames flex less during use and thus take less energy to push up hills) reducing your machine's weight will improve its ability to climb as well. Rotating weight is the real key so you will see the biggest gains from reductions in this area. Use the lightest rims, pedals and shoes you can afford. Tires with smoother and thinner treads and stronger sidewalls will also help.

Improving Lactate Threshold

Lactate threshold is the point at which lactic acid begins to accumulate above moderate levels, resulting in fatigue in the affected muscles. This quickly results in the inability to continue to perform at this level of work. Most riders know the heavy legged feeling after a hard bout of work when you must slow down in order to keep going. The goal of training is to raise the point at which lactic acid accumulates enough to affect performance. All things being equal, the higher your lactate threshold, the faster the pace you can hold on climbs. While lactate threshold can be measured directly it correlates well with heart rate and is normally between 75-90% of maximum heart rate. The goal of climbing-specific training should be to increase that percentage towards the top of the range. A simple way to estimate your lactate threshold is to perform two bouts of work. When rested and motivated and after a good warm-up, perform a twenty minute time trial at **maximum** effort and record your average heart rate. Repeat this test under similar conditions. The average heart rate for both efforts is a close approximation of your heart rate at your lactate threshold. Providing you have a sufficient aerobic endurance base (see 'Build a Base' above) lactate threshold training should improve your climbing ability. This is very demanding training however and will require proper recovery between bouts so don't forget to include easy days on the bike when needed.

Interval Routines

A very effective way to increase your power and to raise your lactate threshold in order to improve climbing ability is through the use of intervals. Intervals are relatively short bursts of more intense effort followed by a recovery period. Several of the below routines should be interspersed (start at the top of the below list and progress down) within your regular riding training (1-3 times per week) depending upon the season. Use them more frequently for pre-season training; tapering off before races. Add/delete routines as needed. Recovery between intervals should be easy, high cadence spinning on mostly level ground.

Big gear climbs - On various hill grades shift up one cog from normal (harder gear) for 1-2 minutes. Keep cadence at least 50 RPM and stay seated.

Cruise intervals - 3 to 5 intervals for 6-12 minutes each on a moderate grade (3-5%) at or just below your lactate threshold. Recover for 2-4 minutes. Gradually add minutes to each interval.

Anaerobic endurance intervals - 3-5 intervals for 2-4 minutes each on a 6-8% grade, gradually building the intensity, with cadence of at least 60 RPM. Intensity should be above your lactate threshold for the second half of the interval. Recovery should be double the interval length.

Extended Climbing at Lactate Threshold - On a steady and moderate grade, climb for 15-30 minutes at or just slightly above your lactate threshold. Gradually add minutes up to 30 (or the longest hill you may need to climb).

Sit/Stand intervals - On a moderate hill and at a comfortable cadence, alternate seated and standing climbing of equal intervals. After thirty seconds in the saddle, stand on the pedals for 30 seconds. After another minute of climbing in the saddle, stand for one minute, etc. Gradually build the intervals up to 4-5 minutes each.

Hill Sprints - Perform 5-10 sprints for 10-15 seconds at maximum effort. Gradually move from moderate to steeper hills. Recover for five minutes between each sprint.

Hill Jumps - While climbing a moderate hill do 4-5 sets of 3-5 jumps for ten crank turns (both feet) at maximum effort. Recover for one minute between each jump and five minutes between each set.

Advanced Hill Jumps - On a moderate grade perform 3-5 two minute sets, attacking every thirty seconds for ten pedal strokes. Stand for the attacks which should be at maximum effort; stay seated otherwise. Recover for five minutes between sets.

Weight Training

One factor linked to climbing success is leg strength. Particularly if you cannot put in year round riding on hills, weight training sessions should be added to your weekly routine. Ideally hit the weight room 2-3 times per week in the off season and once per week in season, tapering off before races or big rides. Increasing upper body strength has the potential to reduce upper body fatigue and increasing lower body strength will give you the ability to push a bigger gear over the same hill. The below exercises will give you the most benefit for your time spent in the gym. Do not include both squats and leg presses unless leg strength is a very weak area. Masters riders or those with lower back issues should not include squats in their routine and should perform the leg press instead.

Squat - 2-3 sets of 8-12 repetitions

Leg press - 2-3 sets of 8-12 repetitions

Calf raise - 2-3 sets of 8-12 repetitions

Step-ups - 2-3 sets of 8-12 repetitions

Bench press - 2-3 sets of 8-12 repetitions

Lat pulldown - 2-3 sets of 8-12 repetitions

Push-ups - 2-3 sets of 25 repetitions

Sit-ups (crunches) - 2-3 sets of 25 repetitions

Back extensions - 2-3 sets of 25 repetitions

Descending

Descending ability, like any other skill, is best obtained and improved with practice. The more time you can spend on descending, the more confidence and speed you will be able to develop. The most important aspect of descending is relaxation. Anxiety can narrow your concentration and you may end up missing a dangerous aspect of the road ahead. Speed is obviously important but pushing your speed to the point of fear will not help your descending skills. Work on relaxation and speed will follow. Keep a slight bend in the arms and slide back in the saddle, keeping your hands on the drops of your bars. One important riding habit to develop is to look far enough in front of you to match the pace at which you are descending. During a faster descent you need to watch the road much further in front of the bike. Set up well in advance of a curve and do whatever braking needs to done before entering the turn. If you are riding in a group, spread out. This will allow each rider to take their preferred line through the corners; critical in that you may not have time to adjust once you commit. It also allows a greater margin if a rider needs to brake. For long descents you should use both brakes equally. Once in a turn any traction used for braking significantly reduces the traction available for cornering. In wet conditions the distance required to stop is extended. Lightly apply the brakes periodically on a wet descent to remove excess water from the rims. Compete only against yourself on a fast descent and exercise caution on unfamiliar roads by always being prepared for road debris or traffic around every blind corner. In many cases descents are followed by another climb; if so, try to spin the pedals as you approach the bottom so that you will be warmed up for the next section of riding. Take it easy,

Tough conditions on GA's Hogpen Gap

Tough descending ahead

33

relax, concentrate on the road, and most importantly, practice descending, and you will find your skills improving.

Mental Training

As professional cyclist Chris Boardman once said "The best climbers do not suffer less, they just suffer faster". Climbing is painful, suffering the name of the game. That said there may also be some less conventional ways to improve your climbing ability. Developing mental focus to enable one to block out distractions, including physical discomfort, is another attribute of good climbers and should be included in your training regimen. All negative thoughts must go during workouts or races. The minute you think you cannot make a climb is when you may get dropped. Many riders are dropped on climbs before they reach their physical breaking point simply because of negative thoughts.

Begin working on mental focus by clearing your mind entirely. This can be a difficult skill to master but can be developed in stretches during long rides. Be patient as it sometimes takes time to see progress. Once this skill is developed begin to think of a single thought or image. Try to keep this single thought or image in your mind for extended periods. Once you have developed this ability you will find it much easier to concentrate over a climb. Work on visualizing images of light or soaring objects as you work your way up the hill. These images can lower the perception of effort. Even if climbing times are similar the effect should be one of additional energy for the remainder of the race or ride. Remember, everyone suffers on a tough climb. Climbing can be as much a mental as physical challenge, so try not to let a lack of self-confidence affect your performance. Developing ways to deal mentally with the physical aspects of getting over tough hills should produce better results on the road.

Climbing Tactics

There are some specific strategies regarding climbing that can have dramatic results when it comes to better race finishes. First of all, as with the overall route, it pays to be very familiar with the climbs along the way, so scout major hills if at all possible, noting the position of flat or very steep sections, particularly those that are stage/race finishes. When many inexperienced riders come to a hill they simply go all out and feel tremendous pressure to reach the top. Unless it is the last climb of the day doing so results in spending enormous amounts of energy that could be saved for the finish. Until you are a great climber you should maintain your own pace. Trying to stay with the top climbers is not good strategy. Instead try to find the exact personal pace that will help you cut your losses. Never ride faster than you know you can go. If needed, as you get comfortable with the climb, see if you can pick up the pace over the last half so that by the top you can catch the original group with which you started. You may be surprised by how many riders you pass along the way. Ideally try to time the effort so that you catch the pack at the summit. Unless you are the first over the top, be careful not to slow down near summits that are not race finishes. As the leaders begin to accelerate on the descent each rider has to push harder over the top in order to hold the wheel in front of him. Shift into a bigger gear as you approach the summit and accelerate over the top. You can recover on the descent from the extra effort involved.

Riders who are good sprinters often come to a hill in or near the lead and then drift to the back of the pack during the climb. On the descent and any following flats they can often catch the lead group before the next climb. By doing this several times early in a ride/race you can save a lot of energy for the finish while also developing the confidence of knowing that you do not have to crest climbs near the front to be successful. If the climb is the last of the day, obviously your tactics will need to change. You may need to make an all out effort to catch the lead group such as when the finish is very close or if being with the group will save a lot of energy (long, flat section just ahead). As you gain experience and become more aware of group dynamics you will start to make better decisions earlier in a climb and save energy as well.

Once you become a good climber, attack on the hills. Use your strength to put time on your competitors as you may need it over the remainder of the race/ride. An early attack can keep pressure on those who may be stronger in other areas. Riders that push too hard trying to keep up with you on a hill early in the race may find themselves struggling on the last climb of the day. Steeper sections are often a good place to launch an attack as you can more quickly open a gap before other riders react. However, attacking early on a hilly stage is a risky decision as you will either ride to victory or go down in flames if the peloton swallows you up before the finish. Depending on the result your decision will be portrayed as courageous or foolish bravado so if you go make sure you are committed to the move. Many a cyclist has made a name for themselves breaking away on a monster climb and staying away so don't let a prior failed attempt keep you from trying again.

If the race finish is the hill crest obviously it is best to be out in front by a comfortable margin and cruise to victory up the final climb. However, until you are a super climber that situation may rarely present itself. Unless it is a very long climb get into the lead group as soon as possible. Once there, knowing when to attack is a crucial skill to master. Much of your decision will be based on how you are feeling that day and on race conditions and will become clearer with additional climbing/racing experience. The other contending riders may also come into play. If there is a sprinter in the lead group you may want to go early and take his legs out from under him. If so, take a measured approach. Launch an attack but not an all out effort. Even though part of the group may stay with you, the effort should drop a few riders. If you are feeling good continue the attack. If you are able to continue at a relatively high cadence you should drop all but the strongest climbers. Unless you have ridden all riders off of your wheel it will come down to your placement in the group and timing as the finish line draws near. The first thing you must do is know where the finish line is. If you scouted the hill even if the last section is twisty with obscured views you should have an advantage. Once you have a good idea of how far away the line is, positioning will be key. Draft off other riders as much as possible as you approach the summit. When the finish is in sight try to be the second or third wheel before the final sprint begins. Realize this is easier said than done and knowing how to position within the group will again come from experience. The time to start your finishing sprint will depend upon your sprinting ability. The greater your sprinting skills, the earlier you can launch your assault. Always be alert for the rider in front of you moving first. Come out of the saddle on the down stroke as you make your move. Once you pull away try to stay directly in front of the rest of the pack so they will have to move around you to pass. Don't look back as you power toward the line. All of these actions should be thought out well before the actual finishing stretch. Many of these tactical maneuvers come with experience so train with experienced riders to see how they approach climbs, or shadow a particular rider, noting how they adjust to different situations on the hill.

Summary

To get the most out of the time on your bike and to avoid over-training refer to the below summary:

- Build a strong aerobic base before adding a lot of climbing mileage to your training rides

- Add climbing to your regular training rides

- Utilize interval training to improve climbing ability

- Build up the intensity of your training slowly

- Train consistently for best results

- Eat a balanced diet

- Try to get a minimum of eight hours sleep every night

- Set short, medium and long-term goals

- Use a training diary and review when needed

- Know yourself and adjust your workouts accordingly

- Don't forget to include easy days on the bike if you are including extensive climbing routines in your training

- Use mental techniques to develop positive thoughts during climbing
- Practice descending skills to round out your mountain training
- Don't forget the tactical side of climbing

The very scenic Big Mountain Road in Virginia

Memorable Climbing Performances

There have been many amazing climbing performances over the years, the most publicized having taken place in Europe. These performances are too numerous to list here and are well documented in other places. From the dominating mountain stage wins of Alfredo Binda, Gino Bartali, Fausto Coppi and Charly Gaul in the early European tours to the death of Tim Simpson on Mont Ventoux and other more contemporary battles among the legends of the sport including Eddy Merckx, Bernard Hinault, Greg Lemond, Marco Pantani and Lance Armstrong, there are many stories to tell. Exclusively American climbing exploits have a fairly short, but accomplished history, mainly contained within the last thirty years or so. The stories presented here have an American theme (either by rider or location) and while some are well known many may be unknown to all but the most die-hard cycling fan.

There are so many tales to tell that all cannot be expanded upon, including some of the early Red Zinger/Coors Classic stage race battles in the Rockies, European race exploits such as Greg Lemond's wins in the 1980 Circuit de la Sarthe and 1983 World Championship, Alexi Grewal's mountain stage win in the 1984 Tour de l'Avenir, the 1986 and 1987 Tour of Switzerland wins over difficult terrain by Andy Hampsten, and the Blue Ridge and Appalachian Mountain performances in the now defunct Tour du Pont. Others worthy of mention but not included in these pages are the victories by Moninger,

Vaughters and Wherry in the now defunct Red Zinger/Saturn Classic, one of the most difficult one day races in the world (held in Colorado from 2000-2002), Lance Armstrong's uphill time trial win to capture the 2001 Tour of Switzerland, his queen (most difficult) stage win in the 2001 Tour de France that gave him the overall race lead or the two mountain stage victories that contributed mightily to his 2002 TdF win. In addition, the exploits of climbers in the recently inaugurated Everest Challenge, a two day stage race in California that has the greatest elevation to mileage ratio for any U.S. race, are not touched upon as well as many others due to lack of space or detailed information. Listed chronologically, those listed here are performances that are among the most significant in American cycling climbing history.

Top of the World

Mount Evans in Colorado is one of the most difficult hill climbs in the world. With a beginning elevation well above 7000 feet, the paved road on its slopes reaches heights greater than any outside of the Himalayas or Andes Mountains. It is also home to the oldest climbing race in the U.S., first held in 1962. Winning this very difficult race, with its unparalleled altitude attained, is a testament to climbing ability. The winner list is one of great American climbers and includes Alexi Grewal, Ned Overend, Jonathan Vaughters, and Tom Danielson. One win in this prestigious event would be a worthy achievement for any top level rider. Multiple wins signify a truly great climber. Winning the overall title each time it was held from 1975-1980, American Bob Cook also set the course record four times in that span. Tragically, Bob Cook passed away in 1981 at the age of twenty-three. The race is now named in memorial for the first five time winner of the event who many consider perhaps the best American climber of any era. Mike Engleman also won the race five times in a row from 1991 to 1995, an equally incredible feat. Scott Moninger has won this race an amazing six times which is quite an achievement. Winning this difficult race multiple times deserves to be considered among the most impressive of climbing feats.

Rocky Mountain High

The Coors Classic (formerly the Red Zinger Classic) was America's first top level stage race and one of the most influential cycling events on this continent. Attracting the world's best riders, it allowed many Americans to see top flight competitive cycling for the first time. Held mainly in Colorado, it always contained many hill climbs within a high altitude environment. In the 1981 version the top team entered was from the Soviet Union. Even though they were technically an amateur team (members did not receive any prize money but were fully supported by the Soviet government and thus could train full time) they were as good as the best professional teams of that era. This was evident in the precise teamwork of its cyclists. Once the Soviet train got moving and was working at its peak it was riding everyone off of its wheels. However, there was one exception. A young man from Nevada who was just starting to make waves in the cycling world was also entered in the Coors Classic that year. Having won several prestigious American titles, he was able to stay with the Soviets, and any other riders for that matter, through the difficult terrain. Greg Lemond, despite having a weak team, stayed with the mighty Soviets throughout the high altitude rides and climbs of the Rockies, pulling ahead at the end of several stages to win. Essentially winning the race single handedly, his impressive mountain performance was a prelude to major tour victories on cycling's most hallowed grounds.

The Future

The Tour de l'Avenir (Tour of the Future) held in France each year is a 10-day stage race sponsored by the Tour de France for top amateurs and young professional riders. It is also similar to the TdF in that it contains plenty of climbing and top flight competition. In 1982 the field was one of the strongest ever including the best national teams in the world along with some of the top up and coming European pros. In addition, a team from Columbia was entered that contained some of the best climbers on the planet. The team from East Germany dominated the early, flat stages but things began to change in Stage 4. This stage was a short mountain time trial and it was here that that the future arrived as American Greg Lemond rode to victory, picking up eighteen seconds on the second place rider. The next day's stage was a brutal one including climb after climb along the route and ending with a hilltop finish. The Columbian team attacked early and often but Lemond followed each one. Toward the end of the stage he opened up a gear that would later be seen winning the Tour de France as he pulled away from everyone and crushed the stage, winning by over five minutes. Greg Lemond ended up winning the Tour de l'Avenir by more than ten minutes, becoming the first and only American ever to do so and building on a record that would become one of the best in the history of the sport.

The Women's Movement

In 1984 the Tour de France held the first Tour for women. Because of the Olympics being held in Los Angeles later that summer the U.S. did not send an official team (and its best riders) to the event. Instead a bicycle club from New Jersey sent a small group to represent the country. Without a coach or national uniforms (they also rode on borrowed bikes) the group headed to France not without a bit of trepidation. Once the race began over mostly flat stages, the Tour was dominated by a strong Dutch team. The last rider picked for the American effort, Marianne Martin, used these early stages to ride herself into top shape. By the time Stage 14 rolled around Martin was ready to make her move. The stage was a difficult one, essentially one long hill and ending at the top of a ski resort. Martin pulled away right from the start and went on to win the stage by almost four minutes, an amazing margin of victory considering the stage was only twenty miles long. Picking up the yellow jersey as race leader as well at the end of that day, she held on all the way to Paris to become the first winner of the Tour de France Feminin.

Conquering the Colombian Heights

Despite its endemic poverty and violence, the country of Colombia, with its towering mountains, has somehow managed to produce a storied cycling history. With some of the toughest riding conditions in the world it is a very inhospitable place for foreign riders; rebuffing even the great Fausto Coppi late in his career. Full of very high elevation passes as well as many of the best climbers in the world (in fact, Colombian Luis Herrera is the only rider to win the King of the Mountains title outright in all three major tours), Colombia held the annual Caracol de la Montana stage race and billed it as the unofficial world championship of climbing. In 1985, battling the altitude and humidity, American Andy Hampsten put in a amazing climbing performance, beating the conditions and competition to come away with the race victory and continuing a series of major American climbing exploits against the best riders in the world.

The American Advance

By 1986 the great French rider, Bernard Hinault, had won five Tours de France and was the dominant rider of his generation. After publicly stating that he would support Greg Lemond in the 1986 TdF, Hinault held a one minute lead on his young teammate in that year's race entering the Pyrenees Mountains. The next day Hinault attacked, and Lemond, very frustrated in the domestique role, could not follow, giving up almost another five minutes by the end of the stage. The following day started as a repeat of the previous one as Hinault again went to the front. On the last climb of the day the race leaders, including Hinault and Lemond, were in the lead group. Multiple attacks were launched and this time Lemond did not hold back. With help from teammate Andy Hampsten, Lemond broke away early on the climb and, pulling away from Hampsten, crushed the stage, picking up almost all of the time he had lost to Hinault the day before. Showing he was now the best rider in the world, Lemond went on to win the Tour, becoming the first American to do so.

Italy Finally Falls

The Giro d'Italia is Italy's grand cycling tour. With a storied history it is the second most difficult race in the world to win. Italy has perhaps the toughest road climbs in Europe but if not, it certainly has more difficult climbs to include in its stages compared to the other major tours, and they are often put to good use. In 1988, Andy Hampsten was riding well as the Giro began. After a solid finish in the opening stage time trial the American hung around until the hills, gradually moving up in general classification. On Stage 12, the first with a hill finish, Hampsten won and put himself very close to the overall lead. The Giro was in the mountains at this point and Stage 14 would be a turning point. The big climb on that stage was up Gavia Pass, a very high, steep and difficult hill. In a pouring rain the peloton stayed together until the base of the Gavia and at that point no one knew what awaited up above on its cruel slopes. As the riders attacked the hill the rain turned to sleet and then to snow near the top. Hampsten stayed with the lead group as riders were shredded around him by the hill and the weather, many abandoning the stage. Hampsten, familiar with the conditions from his training days in Colorado, gritted his teeth and kept pumping the pedals, eventually finishing second in the stage but taking the overall race lead and putting all but one rider minutes behind him in the general classification. He survived multiple attacks over the last week of the race and then won the mountain time trial at the end to cruise to victory, becoming the first and only American to win the Giro d'Italia.

To Descend One Must Climb

After Greg Lemond's dominating win in the 1986 Tour de France the terrible story of his hunting accident is well known, an event that kept him off the bike and on the sidelines for nearly two years. Who knows what his already solid legacy may have been had he been healthy (and had he not had to endure several TdFs as a domestique to the great Bernard Hinault). With his performance capacity obviously diminished after the accident, he put on an amazing time trialing exhibition to win the 1989 Tour, performing well but not superbly in the mountains. In the 1990 TdF the same circumstances were present; Lemond was fit and able but still not quite his old self. The days of his physical domination over, he would need to win races not by brawn but by brains and will. Heading into the key stage in the Pyrenees just over halfway through the race, Lemond found himself behind Italy's Claudio Chiappucci by almost three minutes. As the mountain stages were almost over it was now or never if an assault on a third TdF was to be undertaken. The stage contained three giant climbs lined up over the last half of the route. Chiappucci attacked right at the base of the first climb and flew away, opening a big lead at the summit and increasing it, halfway up the next climb, the mighty Tourmalet, to over three minutes for the stage and almost six minutes overall. Realizing that a critical point had been reached, Lemond launched a severe attack up the Tourmalet, halving the gap to Chiappucci by the summit. The descent of the Tourmalet is a long one, twisting down through very dangerous turns. Always known as a good bike handler, Lemond came down the Tourmalet like a bat out of hell and by the bottom had caught Chiappucci! Making up a gap of one and a half minutes on a descent over another top professional bike rider is an amazing feat, and highlights the importance of descending in mountain stages. However, while catching the stage leader was a heroic effort there were still over eight miles of climbing yet to come before the finish and Chiapucci still had a large overall race lead. The small leading group headed up the final hill and stayed together over much of the final climb. With two miles remaining to the summit however another rider in the group attacked and Lemond went with him, dropping Chiappucci. The smaller group drove hard to the finish, dropping all but two riders by the end (Lemond and future five time TdF winner Miguel Indurain). By the finish Lemond had picked up almost three minutes on the race leader, cutting the overall lead to five seconds, a margin he could easily pick up during the last time trial stage before the race finish in Paris. Going on to win his third TdF, Lemond won the race on the slopes of the Pyrenees with an amazing climbing performance.

The Alp

First used in the Tour de France in 1952, L'Alpe d'Huez, with its multiple, numbered switchbacks, has become one of the most recognizable climbs in the world. Often used as a stage finish, the climb may be the true symbol of the Tour as decisive moments are often played out on its slopes. Almost mythic in stature, all of cycling's greats have done battle there and winning a stage atop the legendary Alp has become one of the most revered accomplishments in cycling. While certainly performing well at the highest level of the sport, Andy Hampsten came to the 1992 TdF without a top level result that matched the climbing exploits that led to his 1988 win in the Giro d'Italia. The Alps that year contained perhaps the most difficult stage of the race, containing four major climbs and ending on top of L'Alpe d'Huez. Feeling well that day, something stirred in Hampsten as he ascended the third climb of the day. Breaking away in a small group, they opened a gap on the field and descended toward L'Alpe. By the base of the climb the group had a four minute lead on everyone else. By the first of many hairpin turns Hampsten was alone. Using an increasingly larger gear he charged up the hill through the huge crowds, gradually pulling away and winning the stage. By conquering the legendary climb he joined cycling's legends on perhaps its most prized summit.

Mount Washington Falls

Mount Washington in New Hampshire may be the toughest climb in the world, with an average grade of almost 12% and portions of the route unpaved. The climb is a brutal one with no flats or descents to catch your breath and riders must often battle cold temperatures and howling winds. An annual hill climb race has been held on its slopes for many years, with the record for the climb having been set way back in 1980. The record stood for seventeen years until a young professional rider, Tyler Hamilton, arrived in 1997 and crushed the competition, lowering the record by almost six minutes in the process, a huge percentage decrease. The record has been lowered subsequently by small margins but Hamilton set the stage and drew attention, as well as some of the world's top riders, to what now may be the most coveted prize in American cycling climbing.

Ventoux

Often used in stage races, Mont Ventoux is a beast of a climb, perhaps the most difficult in France. Soon after the climb begins the trees and most vegetation disappear and riders are left stuck in a barren, parched moonscape that seems to sap the energy of anyone that moves through it. Often used in major European races such as the Dauphine Libere, a major stage race held the month before the Tour de France, Mont Ventoux is a climb that is feared by all riders. Many use the Dauphine as preparation for the Tour so Ventoux has been graced by all of cycling's greats through the years with many a heroic battle having been fought on its slopes, including the death of pro Tom Simpson in 1967 and a memorable duel between Lance Armstrong and Marco Pantani in the 2000 Tour de France. In fact the mountain became Armstrong's nemesis as he failed to win a race that ended on its slopes. The record for the climb had been set way back in 1955 by the great Charley Gaul, a TdF and Giro d'Italia winner with the nickname 'the angel of the mountains'. In 1999 the Dauphine included a time trial up Ventoux for Stage 3. As horrible as the mountain is within the peloton, it is even worse during a time trial. All alone against the hill, riders must dig deep and find an unaided way to the top. American Jonathan Vaughters came to the starting gate that day feeling pretty good. A very successful pro, he entered the stage close to the overall lead and felt a big move on Ventoux could be the difference between winning and losing the race. Vaughters attacked the hill from the beginning, gradually putting time on his opponents at each time check and won the stage, breaking the 44-year-old record for the climb.

A New Beginning

Many questions surrounded Lance Armstrong when the 1999 Tour de France began, including his ability to compete for one, having come back to the sport after a vicious battle with cancer

North Carolina's Beech Mountain

Georgia's Brasstown Bald

(although that question had been answered with some success in pre Tour races). A second question was his ability to climb. A big time trial win early in the race had given him the overall lead as the peloton headed into the Alps. Skeptics were noting however that it was very unlikely that the American could continue his success into the big mountains of the tour. Never a great climber before his illness surely he would succumb once the roads tilted upward. The ninth stage of that year's race was a brutal one. It included six major climbs including the beyond category Galibier in France and Sestrieres in Italy, hallowed ground where all of cycling's greats had battled over the years. To make things worse the weather was poor that day so that the upper altitudes were shrouded in cold and wet weather. In the small lead group at the base of the last climb of the day were many of the best climbers in the race. As they ascended, several fell away so that only four remained. With three miles to go Armstrong attacked, opening a small gap. As the gap grew he poured it on in such a way that no one could respond, pulling away to win the stage by thirty-one seconds and widening his race lead over the top contenders to an almost insurmountable margin. Having dropped almost fifteen pounds and recovered his power since his illness, Armstrong had turned himself into a climbing machine. If there was any doubt regarding his abilities to climb the biggest mountains it was now gone as he went on to win his first TdF.

It Was No Fluke

Before the 2000 Tour de France many cycling pundits felt that Lance Armstrong's 1999 Tour win was a fluke of sorts. With several of the best riders absent that year they reasoned, he would be unlikely to repeat as champion in 2000 when the field included all of the top contenders. As the 2000 event got underway Lance soon found himself down by a wide margin in the overall classification and with a small lead over those considered his strongest competition. A few days later the Tour entered the mountains for the first time and with that a chance for riders to make a big move on the leader board. As the last climb of the day got underway in cold and rainy conditions up the Hautacam, a tough climb in the Pyrenees Mountains, the leading group contained many race contenders with several of them out ahead due to an early breakaway. Soon the group was attacked by 1998 Tour winner Marco Pantani, one of those absent from the 1999 Tour. Armstrong quickly closed the gap, in the process dropping several, among them Jan Ullrich, the 1997 TdF winner and another rider absent in 1999. Even on a very strong day it is a difficult thing for a cyclist to push an attack early on a climb. It is best to wait to see what shakes out as the finish line gets closer. An early attack is considered either foolish bravado or a heroic act depending upon the outcome. However, on that day Armstrong's instincts proved the better of conventional cycling wisdom. Once he had caught and passed Pantani he actually picked up the tempo and pulled away. The rest of the group could not respond and disappeared backward as Lance flew up the mountain. Continuing to charge to the finish line in a steady rain Armstrong caught all but one of the early breakaway riders. But more importantly he had put serious time on all of the top contenders, picking up anywhere from three to five minutes on each. While there was much more riding to be done, the Tour was essentially over and Armstrong had answered one more question.

Changing of the Guard Delayed

Jeannie Longo, an eleven time world champion, came to New Hampshire from France in 2000 looking for a different kind of challenge. Up against the defending women's champion, 18-year-old Genevieve Jeansson of Canada, and perhaps the hardest climb on earth, Mount Washington, Longo knew that she had her work cut out for her during the annual hillclimb race up its slopes. As the race begun, Jeansson took a forty second lead at the two mile mark as the climb headed into its steepest miles. Longo's experience began to show however as she gradually picked up the pace, catching Jeansson at four miles and opening a gap. Jeansson fought back and attacked but she could not quite close to the leader. Longo pulled away, opening a two minute lead and, in what is one of the most amazing climbing performances of all time, at forty-one years of age, won the race, passing all but the two top men and setting the women's record for the hill in the process.

The Look

In the 2001 Tour de France Lance Armstrong, having won the previous two Tours, was in a battle with German rider Jan Ullrich, a former Tour winner and his biggest threat to another victory, as the race entered the first mountain stage. The stage contained three beyond category climbs, ending on the top of the third, the famous L'Alpe d'Huez. Over the first two monster climbs, the Col de la Madeleine and the Col du Glandon, Armstrong struggled just to stay at the back of the lead group. At the beginning of the climb up L'Alpe, Ullrich and several teammates led the way. Suddenly Armstrong shot to the front, pulled there by his teammate Jose Luis Rubiero. As Rubiero pulled off and with Ullrich on his wheel, Armstrong came out of the saddle, and in a moment that has become one of the greatest in cycling history, turned to look back at his competition for a long moment, and accelerated away. Ullrich and the rest of the field had no response and Armstrong won the stage, picking up two minutes on his main rival on the way to his third Tour victory and further cementing his place in the folklore of cycling history.

Redemption

Perhaps driven by her loss to Jeannie Longo of France two years before, Canadian Genevieve Jeansson came to Mount Washington in 2002 with something to prove. The annual hillclimb race up its slopes is perhaps the most brutal on earth but no doubt having lost the event to someone more than twice her age in 2000 must have been incentive enough to draw her back again. She exploded up the hill right from the start, putting time on all of her competition. The road up Mount Washington never wavers and neither did Jeansson that day as she continued her torrid pace all the way to the top, winning the race by a margin of over ten minutes and breaking the hillclimb record previously held by Longo by over four minutes. Only two male riders finished ahead of her as she set a standard that has not since been approached and may be difficult to surpass.

The 'Off' Year

2003 is a year that Lance Armstrong and cycling fans will not forget. It was the year that almost wasn't; the year that Lance could be beaten. Struggling somewhat through the first half of the race Armstrong found himself with a slim lead as the first individual time trial approached. His lead due mostly to a winning team time trial performance, even Armstrong himself knew that something wasn't quite right that year. His pulls were not quite as they had been in years past and his race leading margin showed it. In the time trial Armstrong suffered, whether from mistakes or lack of preparation, and German Jan Ullrich, Lance's chief rival and in second place overall, did what had not been done in a major tour since 1996 as he put hurt and time on the Texas rider and trimmed his slim overall race lead to seconds. Armstrong looked like a beaten man and with only a fifteen second lead most believed that this was the time that he would finally fall as the tour headed into the Pyrenees and the toughest stage of the tour. Containing a category 1 and two beyond category climbs this would be the last chance for the race contenders to take time out of one another before the final time trial. After multiple attacks the second to last climb of the day, the Tourmalet, was descended. At the bottom, the lead group (with one rider several minutes ahead) was a strong one as it started up the Luz-Ardiden to finish the stage. As the group began the brutal climb among tightly packed fans along the route, Armstrong's handle bar caught an obstruction among the spectators, throwing him hard to the ground. Once back up and struggling to restart, his foot detached from his pedal, causing another delay. The lead riders, having moved ahead, slowed in order for the Texan to get back into the climb but much momentum had been lost. Almost immediately after the excitement, the group reformed and Spanish rider Iban Mayo attacked, opening a small gap. After over 100 miles of hard riding and having to remount after hitting the pavement, just finishing the stage would have been considered a victory. Following an attack at that point would seem to be impossible. However, Armstrong immediately jumped the gap to Mayo and, sensing an opportunity, attacked himself. No one else could keep his wheel as he pulled away. Maintaining a brutal pace on the steep climb he soon shredded all behind him, including his main rival, Ullrich. Putting his game face on, Armstrong continued to hammer up the hill, soon catching the lead rider and heading for the finish. Sweat pouring off of him, he knew every second counted in this very close race. Picking up a time bonus as he won the stage, Armstrong showed who was still the boss as he gained time on all of his rivals, eventually securing his fifth TdF victory. It was said that this was what Henry Desgrange, the Tour founder, wanted when he added hills to the race route; suffering and victory no matter what the cost!

Mountain Domination

The 2004 Tour de France held great pressure for Lance Armstrong as he tried to become the first six-time winner of the event. While certainly dominant in mountain stages in the past it was as if he had made a conscious decision in the 2004 event to waste no opportunity as he completed the three week race. When the mountain stages appeared, the other riders certainly knew that the Texan was there to win. As the following accounts attest, Lance was giving away nothing that year.

Stage 12

As the 2004 Tour de France finally got to the real mountains (Pyrennes) Armstrong was over five minutes down in the general classification. After a flat first half the stage ended with two tough climbs. In a bunch near the lead at the base of the last climb, La Mongie, what was left of Armstrong's U.S. Postal team pulled the train, gradually wearing out the rest of the group. After his teammates dropped off, Lance responded to an attack, pulled even and then launched an attack himself. Only a few riders are able to stay with him as he headed for the finish. Attacking again Armstrong ended up on the wheel of the only one ahead of him, Italian Ivan Basso. The two pulled away and while certainly looking like he could have taken the stage win, Armstrong settled for second, picking up valuable time on everyone else. If it was a gift, it was certainly the last one of 2004.

Stage 13

The thirteenth stage of the 2004 TdF was the first true mountain stage of the race. After topping six climbs the U.S. Postal team train had reduced the peloton almost to ruins as only a small group was still in contention halfway through the final climb up the beyond category Plateau de Beille. Once the last of his teammates dropped off, the two strongest climbers in the 2004 race were once again going head to head. Working together this time, both Ivan Basso and Armstrong take turns leading up the severe, unrelenting slope through the mass of fans lining the roadway. Higher and higher they climbed through the human sea, each looking for the finish. With under a mile to go Armstrong zipped up his jersey; he would go for it today! With the line in site the Texan accelerated around Basso for the win.

Stage 15

After a transition ride toward the Alps for Stage 14, the peloton headed into the big mountains for Stage 15. While not containing any giant hills the route was packed with challenging climbs. At the base of the last climb the leading group is full of the usual suspects, including of course, Armstrong. The powerful group relentlessly moved up the hill, shredding riders along the way. As the finish line approached, four strong riders were left, those who would make up four of the top five places in the general classification at day's end. Ivan Basso made the first move but Armstrong, timing his attack to perfection, swung under the Italian around a corner to take the stage win, picking up the yellow jersey as the tour leader for the first time in the race.

Stage 16

The climb up L'Alpe d'Huez in the Alps is one of most difficult used in the Tour de France. In the 2004 version, one of the time trial stages was a battle up its slopes. In time trials, riders are all alone, forced to set tempo by themselves, as they start two minutes apart with their starting time determined by their place in the general classification (the last place rider goes first, the first place rider goes last..). Huge crowds lined the route, the largest of the race so far. Over the early phase of the ride Armstrong rode conservatively, and was in ninth place at the first time check. Picking up the pace in the middle of the race, Lance started to make up time, spinning his high cadence style up the slope. Soon another rider appeared in front of him, a target to acquire. It was Basso, his nemesis over the last week, who was getting caught, despite having started a full two minutes ahead! Armstrong pulled even and, not even glancing at his rival, accelerated around a corner and disappeared up the road. His face grim with determination, he continued to put time on every rider. As he crossed the finish line the stage, and the Tour, were all but over. Battling a mass of fans that parted only at the last minute as the riders passed, throwing water, encouragement, epithets and worse, Armstrong put in another amazing climbing performance, winning the stage and picking up additional minutes on all his rivals as he moved toward his record setting sixth TdF win. As Lance said afterwards, "I wanted it bad. I wanted it for the history on the mountain…"

Stage 17

With the GC lead and multiple stage wins at this point, conventional wisdom might have been to take it easy on the last mountain stage; to take no chances and cruise into Paris for the trophy. However, this was 2004 and something was in the air. A very tough day led over three category 1 and one beyond category climbs. The usual scenario played out as a strong group of five riders, including Armstrong, led over the top of the last big climb of the day. After a descent, the finishing stretch was rolling terrain with a slightly uphill finish. Armstrong's teammate, Floyd Landis, was in the lead group, and looking to pick up a stage win. With less than two kilometers to go Landis attacked but everyone went with him and soon he was reeled in. At the one kilometer to go mark the German rider Andreas Kloden suddenly took off from the back of the pack, surprising everyone and opening a big gap. It appeared the stage was his. As he saw

Landis's hopes of winning fading away, Armstrong came out of the saddle and began to sprint. Pulling away from the others he amazingly closed the gap to Kloden in a flash and pulled past the German at the line, winning his third stage in a row. Winning four of five mountain stages (and finishing second in the fifth) Armstrong's performance in the 2004 TdF was one of the most dominating climbing exhibitions ever seen.

Top of the World

As previously mentioned, Mount Evans in Colorado is one of the most difficult climbs in the U.S. With the road soaring to over 14,000 feet, much of its difficulty is due to altitude. The annual race up its slopes always draws many top climbers but by 2004 it had been twelve years since the course record had been assaulted. With snow having fallen the previous day and in cold and foggy conditions, American Tom Danielson put in a spectacular performance as he won the race by an unheard of 8 minutes and 40 seconds, chopping 4 minutes and 10 seconds off of the record. Having been training extensively at altitude and in mid-season form Danielson, one of the best climbers in the world (the current record holder on Mount Washington as of 2006 and multiple other climbs), raised the bar on Mount Evans and set a standard that may be difficult to surpass for some time to come.

The Lieutenant Strikes

Longtime faithful lieutenant to Lance Armstrong but a highly skilled rider in his own right, George Hincapie had never won a Tour de France stage despite numerous one day race wins. Stage 15 of the 2005 TdF was the most difficult of the race, containing four category 1 climbs and one beyond category climb to finish the stage. Getting into a breakaway early, Hincapie fought off many attacks as the stage progressed. Finally, on the last climb of the day, the Pla-d'Adet, Hincapie and Oscar Pereiro, who had done much of the leg work in the breakaway, pulled away from what was left of the leading group as the finish line approached. Marking Pereiro up the cruel steeps, Hincapie stayed behind while looking for the finish line. With 200 hundred meters to go he swung around the Spanish rider who had no response and charged to the hilltop win, becoming one of only a handful of Americans to win a major tour mountain stage.

A Tradition Continues

The 2006 Tour de France was considered wide open after the great one, Lance Armstrong, retired after his 7th straight win. American Floyd Landis came into that year's race well prepared. Having won several prestigious titles that year, he was poised to take over where Lance had left off. Leading the race as it headed into the Alps, Landis bonked on stage 16, losing his lead and much of his dignity in the process. Stage 17, he knew, might be his last chance at ever winning the Tour. It was a tough stage, with multiple difficult climbs along its route. Attacking early, the other riders sat back, thinking a move at this point was suicide. However, Landis knew just was he was doing. He quickly overtook an earlier breakaway group and continued hammering up the hills. Soon he was up by over nine minutes. What was left of the peloton finally woke up and began chasing in earnest. On the final climb of day, the beyond category Col de Joux Plane, Landis blew his last stage challenger off of his wheel and had a five minute lead at the summit. He then picked up an incredible additional 30 seconds on the field during the descent. Gaining over seven minutes on the overall leader that day, he went on to eventually win the TdF. Having attacked for over 80 miles through mountainous terrain, Landis's ride that day was one of the greatest in Tour history.

A distant climb beckons

State Maps of Climbs

Alabama

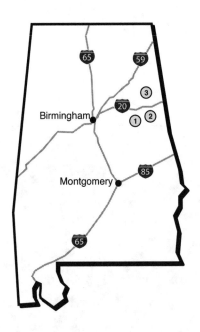

Georgia

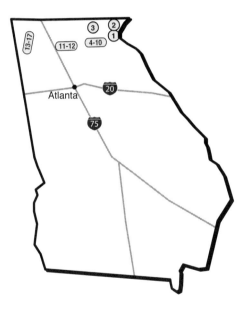

North Carolina

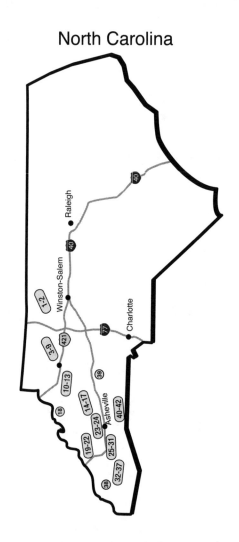

South Carolina

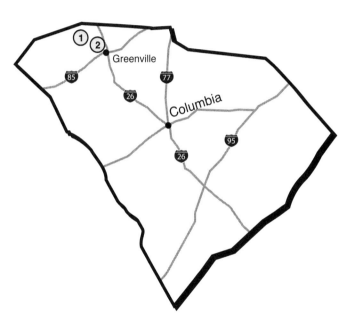

Tennessee

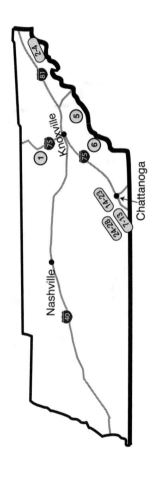

Virginia

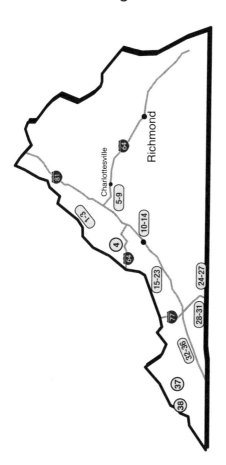

West Virginia

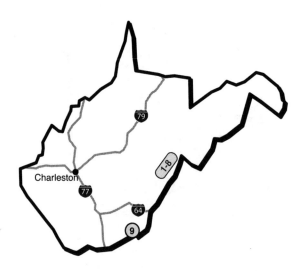

Alabama

Mount Cheaha East

Total elevation - 1,407 ft   **Length - 4.1 miles**
Average Grade - 6.5% (11%)   **Rating - 0.91 (cat 2)**

The highest point in Alabama, Mt Cheaha is a solid climb. At mile 3.3 turn right into the State Park and hit the steepest grade on the climb. The listed climb ends at the marker for the highest point in Alabama.

Directions - Begin the listed climb at the junction of routes 49 and 281 east of Cheaha State Park in east central Alabama by continuing on 281 toward the Park.

Mount Cheaha West

Total elevation - 1,232 ft   **Length - 3.3 miles**
Average Grade - 7.1% (11%)   **Rating - 0.87 (cat 2)**

The other side of Mt Cheaha is an isolated ascent that begins at a small lake within Cheaha State Park. At mile 1.0 turn left on Route 281 and then left again at mile 2.5 and hit the steepest grade on the climb, an identical ending to the previous climb.

Directions - Head north from Talladega, AL on Route 21 for several miles to Route 398 (right). Head east on 398 for several miles to Cheaha Rd on the right. Take Cheaha Rd east for 11 rolling miles into the State Park and the climb begins at the lake.

Chimney Peak

Total elevation - 891 ft	Length - 1.8 miles
Average Grade - 9.4% (20%)	Rating - 0.88 (cat 2)

The ascent of Chimney Peak is along a variable grade in east central Alabama. There is 0.4 miles of double digit grade in the first mile including a max of 20% and then the climb flattens out. It rears up towards climbs end along double digit grade again to finish. A closed gate may keep you off of the final 0.1 miles.

Directions - In the middle of Jacksonville, AL on route 21 head east on Mountain Rd. The climb begins 1.1 miles down Mountain Rd just beyond Englewood Dr on your left.

The very steep Chimney Peak in Alabama

Georgia

28 South

Total elevation - 2,101 ft	**Length - 10.6 miles**
Average Grade - 3.8% (8%)	**Rating - 0.80 (cat 2)**

28 is an isolated climb up to Highlands, NC. After 3.3 miles the road descents to Big Creek and then resumes climbing, ending at the eastern continental divide in Highlands. Never steep, the ascent is a pleasant one mostly within deep woods.

Directions - In Dilliard, GA head east for 7-8 miles on Warwoman Road where it deadends at Route 28. Turn right for 1/10 mile to begin the climb by reversing your course.

246/106

Total elevation - 888 ft	**Length - 2.0 miles**
Average Grade - 8.4% (10%)	**Rating - 0.75 (cat 2)**

A steep ascent with traffic, the listed climb ends after 2 miles at an obvious but unmarked top. You can continue for another 12 miles into Highlands, NC but the route is rolling and shallow along the way.

Directions - In Dillard, GA head north on 441 for several miles to 246 on the right. Head up 246 for 1.6 miles where the climb begins.

Brasstown Bald

Total elevation - 1,824 ft	**Length - 3.1 miles**
Average Grade - 11.1% (21%)	**Rating - 2.24 (cat 1)**

This hill starts out steep along a very tight, twisty road with multiple ramps of 10-15% grade along with a section of 20%. The road comes to an apparent end after 2.5 miles at a parking area. From there you must ride the shuttle van road to the top, a half mile with an average grade of nearly 15% (bikes not allowed; the vans stop running at 6PM during summer). There is a national forest visitor's center on top (the highest point in Georgia) with great views of the surrounding mountains. If taken all the way up this is a tough hill. This climb is often used as a stage finish in the Tour of Georgia (closed in winter - Chattahoochee National Forest - 706 745-6928).

Directions - From Hiawassee, GA head south on route 17/75 for several miles to route 180. Turn right on route 180 and head 5.3 miles to 180 Spur on your right. The climb begins at the intersection of route 180 and 180 Spur.

Hogpen Gap East

Total elevation - 1,431 ft	**Length - 4.1 miles**
Average Grade - 6.6% (9%)	**Rating - 0.95 (cat 2)**

Less steep but longer than its west side, Hogpen Gap East is a nice climb up to the gap. It contains several small flats along the way which lessens its average grade.

Directions - From Helen, GA head south on Alternate 75 to Route 348 on your right. Take 348 for several miles to its unmarked start.

Hogpen Gap West

Total elevation - 1,257 ft	Length - 2.2 miles
Average Grade - 10.7% (13%)	Rating - 1.36 (cat 1)

One of the steepest roads in the US, the west side of Hogpen Gap will test you. Just past Tesnatee Gap is the steepest half mile of the route. From Tesnatee to just before the summit, the rock wall to your right is one of the few places in the SE one can ice climb in the winter.

Directions - From the junction of routes 180 and 348 in tiny Choestoe, GA head east on 348 for 4.9 rolling miles to begin the listed climb.

Wolfpen Gap North

Total elevation - 1,054 ft	Length - 3.1 miles
Average Grade - 6.1% (9%)	Rating - 0.64 (cat 2)

The north side of Wolfpen Gap is a nice climb along an infrequently travelled and twisty road to a signed summit. A solid grade will make you work to get to its top. This is a very pleasant ascent.

Directions - The climb begins at the junction of Routes 129/19 and 180 at Vogel State Park by continuing on 180.

Wolfpen Gap South

Total elevation - 485 ft	Length - 2.1 miles
Average Grade - 4.4% (8%)	Rating - 0.22 (cat 3)

The south side of Wolfpen is a shorter and more shallow way to get to the gap.

Directions - From Suches, GA, take 180 south from Route 60 for 5.8 miles to begin the listed climb.

Neels Gap East

Total elevation - 1,570 ft	Length - 7.0 miles
Average Grade - 4.4 (8%)	Rating - 0.65 (cat 2)

The east side of Neels Gap is a fairly shallow climb along twisty 219/19 with some traffic. The listed stats are estimates.

Directions - The climb begins at the junction of 19 and 219 by heading west on 219/19.

Neels Gap West

Total elevation - 1,101 ft	Length - 5.5 miles
Av erage Grade - 3.8% (8%)	Rating - 0.42 (cat 3)

The west side of Neels Gap is a shallow climb with some traffic along a twisty road that is 3 lanes in places.

Directions - Begin the climb at the junction of 180 and 219 by heading east on 219 toward Neels Gap.

Woody Gap East

Total elevation - 1,281 ft	**Length - 5.4 miles**
Average Grade - 4.5% (9%)	**Rating - 0.58 (cat 2)**

The east side climb to Woody Gap is a pleasant one with good views in places and some traffic. The grade is steady and the climb ends at the Appalachian Trail.

Directions - From Dahlonega, GA head north on Route 19 to route 61 (left) and the listed climb begins at the junction.

Fort Mountain East

Total elevation - 1,394 ft	**Length - 6.4 miles**
Average Grade - 4.1% (8%)	**Rating - 0.58 (cat 2)**

The east side of Fort Mountain is a rolling ascent that ends at an unmarked top several miles shy of the State Park entrance.

Directions - From Elijay, GA head west on Route 52 for several miles to begin the climb.

Fort Mountain West

Total elevation - 1,894 ft	**Length - 6.1 miles**
Average Grade - 5.9% (8%)	**Rating - 1.11 (cat 1/2)**

One of the greatest elevation gained climbs in GA, the west side of Fort Mountain leads to Fort Mountain State Park. Nice views near the top and a steady grade results in a pleasant mountain climb. The listed stats end at the State Park entrance. The road continues to climb intermittently but significant climbing is over.

Directions - In Chatsworth, GA at the junction of routes 76 and 52, head east on Route 52 for 1.2 miles (7th Day Adventist Church on right) to begin the listed climb.

Dougherty Gap

Total elevation - 626 ft	**Length - 1.6 miles**
Average Grade - 7.4% (14%)	**Rating - 0.46 (cat 3)**

A short and steep way to get to the top of the southern end of Lookout Mountain.

Directions - From tiny Cooper Heights, GA on Route 193 head south on 193 for several miles to Cone Rd on the right. Take Cone Rd for 11.4 miles to begin the climb.

136 East

Total elevation - 969 ft	**Length - 3.1 miles**
Average Grade - 5.9% (9%)	**Rating - 0.57 (cat 2/3)**

Another interesting route to the top of Lookout Mountain, 136 East is never steep but its grade is a good workout.

Directions - From tiny Cooper Heights, GA at the junction of routes 193 and 136 head east on 136 for just over a mile to where the listed climb begins.

Nick A Jack Road

Total elevation - 714 ft	**Length - 1.6 miles**
Average Grade - 8.4% (10%)	**Rating - 0.60 (cat 2)**

Another steep and short approach to Lookout Mountain, Nick A Jack's grade will test you. The listed stats end just short of the top of the mountain before a flat/descent.

Directions - From tiny Cooper Heights, GA at the junction of routes 193 and 136 head north on 193 for several miles. Nick A Jack Road will appear on your left. Head down Nick A Jack for 1.2 rolling miles where the listed climb begins.

136 West

Total elevation - 1,248 ft	**Length - 4.2 miles**
Average Grade - 5.6% (9%)	**Rating - 0.70 (cat 2)**

The west side of 136 also takes you to the top of Lookout Mountain on its Georgia side. The grade is solid and steady with some traffic. At mile 4.0 turn left or right on Sunset to get to the very top of the listed climb.

Directions - From Trenton, GA head west on Route 136 where the climb begins shortly near the junction with Piney Rd on the left.

Burkhalter Gap

Total elevation - 1,149 ft   **Length - 2.6 miles**
Average Grade - 8.4% (14%)   **Rating - 0.96 (cat 2)**

Called by some locals the most difficult way to get to the top of
Lookout Mountain, Burkhalter Gap is a tough climb up the west
side of the massive. Steep immediately, it carries a fairly steady
grade and dead ends with Route 157 on top.

Directions - In Trenton, GA head north on Piney Rd from Route
136 in town. Travel Piney Rd for 2.1 miles to where the climb
begins at the point where the grade changes significantly.

Steep Dougherty Gap in Georgia

North Carolina

Pilot Mountain

Total elevation - 1,073 ft   **Length - 2.3 miles**
Average Grade - 8.8% (16%)   **Rating - 0.97 (cat 2)**

This is a steep knob climb within Pilot Mountain State Park. Steep from the start the road is narrow and twisty, running underneath thick trees for much of its route. There is a mile in the middle of the climb that is double digit grade and a parking lot on top with hiking possibilities.

Directions - Take Highway 52 north from Winston-Salem, NC for ~20 miles to the Pilot Mountain State Park exit (right). Turn left at the stop sign and then left again on Pilot Mountain State Park Road. The climb begins here.

Sauratown Mountain

Total elevation - 946 ft   **Length - 2.6 miles**
Average Grade - 6.9% (19%)   **Rating - 0.65 (cat 2)**

This is another knob climb that has challenging sections along its route. Be ready early on this one as there is near 20% grade right at the beginning and a double digit grade section about half-way to the top. The road deadends and is a fun descent.

Directions - Take highway 52 north from Winston-Salem, NC for ~6 miles to Moore/RJR Drive. Turn left at the end of the exit on Moore/RJR and follow it for 4.5 miles (stay straight at all intersections) to Route 66. Go left on 66 for 6.6 miles to Taylor Rd (left). Sauratown Mountain Rd is 0.9 miles down Taylor (on your left).

89/18

Total elevation - 1,131 ft   **Length - 3.4 miles**
Average Grade - 6.3% (8%)   **Rating - 0.71 (cat 2)**

This is a pleasant and challenging climb that carries little traffic. At mile 2.8 turn left on Route 18 and the climb soon ends at the Blue Ridge Parkway.

Directions - From Elkin, NC head north on I-77 for ~20 miles to Route 89. Take Route 89 west for ~10 miles to Goodson Rd (left) where the listed climb begins by continuing up the hill on 89.

21 East

Total elevation - 1,420 ft   **Length - 4.9 miles**
Average Grade - 5.5 (9%)   **Rating - 0.78 (cat 2)**

Route 21 is a pleasant climb along a heavily forested ridge with some traffic that intersects with the Blue Ridge Parkway at its end.

Directions - From I-77 in Elkin, NC head west on Route 21 for ~10 miles to Railroad Grade Rd on the right where the listed climb begins.

16 East

Total elevation - 1,807 ft   **Length - 5.7 miles**
Average Grade - 6.0% (9%)   **Rating - 1.08 (cat 1/2)**

Route 16 is a nice climb up to the Blue Ridge Parkway. A steady grade provides a good workout. You can use this route to make a loop ride using the Parkway and descending parallel Route 18 (next climb) back to North Wilkesboro.

Directions - In North Wilkesboro, NC head west on 421 for several miles to its junction with 16. Turn right on 16 and travel 10.4 miles along 16 to Berrys Branch Road on the right where the listed climb begins.

18 East

Total elevation - 1,590 ft   **Length - 4.4 miles**
Average Grade - 6.7% (8%)   **Rating - 1.10 (cat 1/2)**

Route 18 is very similar to the previous climb (Route 16) although a bit steeper and is a great way to get to the Blue Ridge Parkway. The grade is steady and the route carries some traffic. You can make a nice loop with routes 16 and 18 and the Parkway.

Directions - In North Wilkesboro, NC head north on Route 18 for several miles to Old 18 on the right. The listed climb begins 4.7 miles after old 18 at Long Bottom Rd (significant grade change).

Mount Jefferson

Total elevation - 1,335 ft	**Length - 3.2 miles**
Average Grade - 7.9% (11%)	**Rating - 1.05 (cat 1/2)**

The climb to Mt Jefferson is a steep test and very scenic for much of its route. The first mile contains the steepest climbing but the grade never becomes shallow. There are excellent views at several hairpin turns and the climb ends at a parking area near the top of the mountain.

Directions - The climb begins just south of Jefferson, NC at the junction of Route 221 and Mt Jefferson State Park Rd. The listed stats begin 0.1 mile up Mt Jefferson State Park Rd.

Snake Mountain South

Total elevation - 1,102 ft	**Length - 2.9 miles**
Average Grade - 7.2% (17%)	**Rating - 0.81 (cat 2)**

The south side of Snake Mountain near Boone, NC is a stiff climb up to Elk Knob State Park. The route starts out shallow but increases in grade once you pass Rich Mountain Rd on the left. This last section includes double digit grade and the summit is unmarked but obvious.

Directions - From 421 in Boone, NC head north on Route 94 for ~5 miles to Meat Camp Rd on the left. Head up Meat Camp Road for 2.6 miles and the climb begins at the junction of Meat Camp Rd and Little Creek Road.

Snake Mountain North

Total elevation - 1,052 ft   **Length - 2.7 miles**
Average Grade - 7.4% (10%)   **Rating - 0.79 (cat 2)**

The north side of Snake Mountain is along a solid and steady grade and while it does not contain as steep a stretch as its south side, it is still a worthwhile ascent.

Directions - See Previous climb. At the top of Snake Mountain South descend Meat Camp Rd 2.7 miles to Snyder Branch Rd. The listed climb begins by heading back up the hill.

Hawksnest

Total elevation - 1,521 ft   **Length - 3.8 miles**
Average Grade - 7.6% (16%)   **Rating - 1.15 (cat 1/2)**

The route to Hawksnest is a steep climb with a variable grade near Sugar Mountain, NC. After a steep start through switchbacks, at mile 1.3 bear left to continue on Skyland Drive and the grade eases. At mile 3.0 bear right on SkiView and the grade soon increases to double digits in places. At mile 3.5 the road becomes Tangle Lane and gets very steep for a short stretch. Just before the end turn right on Devine View Court to finish.

Directions - From the junction of routes 184 and 105 south of Boone, NC head north on 105 (toward Boone) for several miles. Seven Devil Rd is on the left and the climb begins at that junction.

Seven Devils

Total elevation - 1,089 ft	**Length - 1.9 miles**
Average Grade - 10.9% (18%)	**Rating - 1.24 (cat 1)**

The route to Seven Devils shares its start with Hawksnest (previous climb) and continues as a very steep ascent. At mile 1.3 turn left on Alpine Drive into a neighborhood and very narrow streets. After 0.1 miles on Alpine begin a series of quick turns (Wildcat Rocks then Rock Cove Court) along double digit grade to finish at a single lane deadend. Be careful descending from here. There are other routes in Seven Devils that climb steeply so explore the area if possible.

Directions - See previous climb.

Beech Mountain

Total elevation - 1,701ft	**Length - 3.5 miles**
Average Grade - 9.2% (17%)	**Rating - 1.66 (cat 1)**

Beech Mountain is a difficult climb that was used as a stage finish in the now defunct Tour DuPont. The first 3 miles contain some double digit grade and big switchbacks. Turn left on Ski Loft Rd at mile 3.1 for a very steep finish (4/10ths mile at 13%). Lance Armstrong used this hill early in his cycling recovery. He and everyone else suffers on this hill.

Directions - In Banner Elk, NC head west on 194 for 3/10ths mile to Beech Mountain Rd (on your right). The listed stats start from the dip in the road just down Beech Mountain Rd (Old Turnpike Rd on the left).

The south side of Snake Mountain in NC

A steep switchback on upper Beech Mtn NC

Roan Mountain South

Total elevation - 2,927 ft	Length - 8.1 miles
Average Grade - 6.8% (9%)	Rating - 2.12 (cat 1)

The south side of Roan Mountain is a solid and difficult climb up to high altitude. A steady grade and good scenery will make for a pleasant ride.

Directions - In Bakersville, NC head north on Route 261 for 6.3 rolling miles to Green Creek Rd (on right in Glen Ayre) to begin.

181 East

Total elevation - 2,663 ft	Length - 12.6 miles
Average Grade - 4.0% (9%)	Rating - 1.09 (cat 1/2)

181 is a long, scenic and shallow climb up to the Blue Ridge Parkway. There is great mountain biking in the area as well.

Directions - In Morganton, NC head north on route 181 to Brown Mountain Beech Road (right). Continue on 181 for another 0.8 miles to Streamside Rd (right) where the listed climb begins.

226 East

Total elevation - 1,377 ft	Length - 4.1 miles
Average Grade - 6.4% (10%)	Rating - 0.88 (cat 2)

226 is a nice climb up to the Blue Ridge Parkway. Never steep its scenery makes it a worthy ascent.

Directions - From Marion, NC head north on 221 to Route 226. 226 will be on your left and the listed climb begins just over 1 mile down 226 at its junction with 226A (left).

226A

Total elevation - 1,955 ft	**Length - 9.7 miles**
Average Grade - 3.8% (8%)	**Rating - 0.76 (cat 2)**

An alternate route up to the Blue Ridge Parkway, 226A is a scenic and shallow ascent.

Directions - From Marion, NC head north on 221 to Route 226. 226 will be on your left. Head up 226 for a short distance and 226A will appear on your left where the listed climb begins.

Mount Mitchell

Total elevation - 5,161 ft	**Length - 24.1 miles**
Average Grade - 4.0% (10%)	**Rating - 2.24 (cat 1)**

Mount Mitchell is the longest climb in this guide and one of the most difficult. It has one of the greatest elevation gains of any climb in the U.S. The first section (route 80) contains many 180 degree switchbacks as it nears the Blue Ridge Parkway. Turn left on the Parkway and travel through several tunnels. After a descent, resume climbing and turn right on Mt Mitchell State Park Road. This final section is a bit steeper and the road deadends near the top of Mount Mitchell at the highest legal road in the eastern US.

Directions - In Marion, NC, at the junction of routes 221 and 70, head south on 70. Go approx two miles and turn right on route 80. After 2.8 miles you come to the Lake Tohoma dam. Circle the lake to the small bridge over the creek that feeds the lake to begin the climb.

226 East (TN border)

Total elevation - 959 ft	Length - 4.3 miles
Average Grade - 4.2% (8%)	Rating - 0.41 (cat 3)

226 East is a very scenic climb that begins near the Toe River and ends on the Tennessee state line on top.

Directions - The listed climb begins in the tiny burg of Buladean, NC on Route 226.

Doggett Gap East

Total elevation - 1,412 ft	Length - 3.1 miles
Average Grade - 8.6% (11%)	Rating - 1.24 (cat 1)

The east side of Doggett Gap is a steep test up to an unmarked summit. Tree lined and scenic, there are 2 big switchbacks along the way that will get your attention.

Directions - In Asheville, NC head west on Route 63 into Madison County. The climb begins 3.7 miles west of the county line just before the road enters the trees.

Doggett Gap West

Total elevation - 1,181 ft   **Length - 3.4 miles**
Average Grade - 6.6% (8%)   **Rating - 0.79 (cat 2)**

The west side of Doggett Gap is a pleasant climb along a steady grade that ends at unmarked Doggett Gap.

Directions - In the tiny burg of Trust, NC at the junction of routes 209 and 63 head east on 63 for 1.7 miles to where the listed climb begins at a left hand turn in the road.

Betsy Gap East

Total elevation - 1,188 ft   **Length - 3.5 miles**
Average Grade - 6.4% (9%)   **Rating - 0.78 (cat 2)**

The east side of Betsy Gap begins in a valley before entering thick woods near its signed top. Never steep, its scenery is its top quality.

Directions - In the tiny burg of Trust, NC at the junction of routes 209 and 63 head west on 209 for 2.7 miles to a creek crossing. The listed climb begins just beyond the creek.

Betsy Gap West

Total elevation - 1,276 ft   **Length - 3.9 miles**
Average Grade - 6.2% (9%)   **Rating - 0.81 (cat 2)**

The west side of Betsy Gap may be the most scenic in the area. Never steep, it is a quality climb that ends at a signed summit.

Directions - From I-40 west of Asheville, NC take Route 209. Travel 209 north for several miles to a junction with Max Patch Rd and Betsy Gap Rd. The listed climb begins at the junction by heading up Betsy Gap Rd.

Craggy Gardens

Total elevation - 2,978 ft   **Length - 16.2 miles**
Average Grade - 3.5% (9%)   **Rating - 1.07 (cat 1/2)**

Craggy Gardens is a shallow and beautiful climb along the Blue Ridge Parkway. At mile 15.0 turn left toward Craggy Gardens along an increased grade.

Directions - In Asheville, NC the climb begins at the junction of Highway 70 and the Blue Ridge Parkway by heading north on the Parkway.

Town Mountain Road

Total elevation - 771 ft   **Length - 1.8 miles**
Average Grade - 8.1% (10%)   **Rating - 0.63 (cat 2)**

Town Mountain Rd is a short but tough climb in Asheville, NC that carries some traffic. At mile 1.4 turn left on Sunset Summit and then at mile 1.6 turn right on Crowning Way to finish at an unmarked summit.

Directions - In Asheville, NC head to the junction of Town

Mountain Rd and Cameron Street (left) near I-240 to begin.

Mount Pisgah

Total elevation - 2,914 ft	**Length - 14.3 miles**
Average Grade - 3.9% (8%)	**Rating - 1.16 (cat 1/2)**

Mt Pisgah is a very scenic climb along the Blue Ridge Parkway. The grade is fairly steady and multiple (9) tunnels need to be negotiated along the way. The first 3 are long enough that they are pitch dark so go prepared.

Directions - Just south of Asheville, NC the climb begins at the junction of Highway 191 and the Blue Ridge Parkway by heading south on the Parkway.

151/Mount Pisgah

Total elevation - 2,340 ft	**Length - 6.1 miles**
Average Grade - 7.3% (10%)	**Rating - 1.75 (cat 1)**

---

151 is a great and scenic climb along a steep grade through thick trees up to the Blue Ridge Parkway near Asheville, NC. Most of its route is very twisty (3.8 miles at 8%). At the Parkway turn right and climb for another 2.3 solid miles through 2 short tunnels to the Mt Pisgah parking area (previous climb).

Directions - In Asheville, NC head west on I-40 for a few miles and go south on Route 19/23. Travel 19/23 for several miles and go left on 151. Travel 151 for 6.5 rolling miles to Chestnut Creek Rd on the right where the listed climb begins.

276 East

Total elevation - 2,244 ft   **Length - 9.9 miles**
Average Grade - 4.3% (8%)   **Rating - 0.99 (cat 2)**

The east side of 276 is a very scenic and shallow climb that carries a fair amount of traffic. Looking Glass Falls will get your attention on your right and the climb ends at the Blue Ridge Parkway.

Directions - Just north of Brevard, NC at the junction of 276 and 64 head west on 276. The listed climb begins 5.4 miles down 276 at its junction with the road to the Pisgah Center for Wildlife Education on your left.

276 West

Total elevation - 1,177 ft   **Length - 3.8 miles**
Average Grade - 5.9% (9%)   **Rating - 0.71 (cat 2)**

The west side of 276 is a solid climb up to the Blue Ridge Parkway along a solid and stead grade. A big switchback will get your attention near its start.

Directions - East of Waynesville, NC head east on 276 from its junction with 215 for 11.7 miles to the Big East Fork Trailhead (right) to begin the listed climb. The road begins climbing before this point but it is intermittent and mostly shallow climbing (but a worthwhile ride).

A warning along 151/Mt Pisgah in NC

The top of 215 South near the Blue Ridge Parkway in NC

215 South

Total elevation - 2,449 ft
Average Grade - 6.0% (9%)

Length - 7.8 miles
Rating - 1.50 (cat 1)

The south side of 215 is a difficult and scenic climb and another route to reach the Blue Ridge Parkway. Trees down below give way to good views up top and the listed climb ends under the Parkway.

Directions - On Route 64 in Brevard, NC head south on 64 for several miles to 215 (right). Head north on 215 for 9.3 rolling miles to Indian Creek Rd on the right where the listed climb begins.

215 North

Total elevation - 2,219 ft
Average Grade - 4.9% (8%)

Length - 8.5 miles
Rating - 1.13 (cat 1/2)

The north side of 215 is a fairly shallow but spectacular climb to the Blue Ridge Parkway that includes a large waterfall about halfway to the top on your right. The grade is never steep and a few cars will likely pass you but not enough to influence your climb.

Directions - In Waynesville, NC head east on 276 for several miles to Route 215. Head south on 215 for ~10 rolling miles to the Sunburst Recreation Area on the right to begin the listed climb.

Cove Creek Road

| Total elevation - 1,228 ft | Length - 3.9 miles |
| Average Grade - 6.0% (9%) | Rating - 0.75 (cat 2) |

Cove Creek Road is a very nice and isolated climb on a narrow road through a sparsely populated neighborhood. Generally getting steeper as you go the listed climb ends where the pavement ends.

Directions - From I-40 west of Asheville, NC head south on Route 276 for several hundred yards to Cove Creek Rd on the right. Travel the road 0.4 miles to begin the listed climb (junction with 284).

Richland Balsam

| Total elevation - 2,690 ft | Length - 11.7 miles |
| Average Grade - 4.4% (9%) | Rating - 1.25 (cat 1) |

Richland Balsam is a nice climb up to the highest elevation on the Blue Ridge Parkway. There is a dark tunnel along the way so be prepared but at least the grade eases after the tunnel. The remainder of the ascent is rolling and the climb ends at an unmarked top with great views.

Directions - The climb begins at the junction of Highway 23/74 and the Blue Ridge Parkway (Soco Gap) by heading north on the Parkway.

Waterrock Knob East

Total elevation - 2,376 ft
Average Grade - 5.2% (8%)

Length - 8.7 miles
Rating - 1.29 (cat 1)

Heading in the opposite direction on the Blue Ridge Parkway as the previous climb, Waterrock Knob is a very scenic ascent along a steady grade. At the top of the ridge turn right to finish at a parking area for Waterrock Knob.

Directions - The climb begins at the junction of Highway 23/74 and the Blue Ridge Parkway (Soco Gap) by heading south on the Parkway.

19 South/Waterrock Knob

Total elevation - 3,580 ft
Average Grade - 5.4% (9%)

Length - 12.6 miles
Rating - 2.03 (cat 1)

Route 19 is a narrow road that carries some traffic. At mile 7.6 turn right onto the Blue Ridge Parkway and continue along one of the most scenic sections of climbing on earth. At the top of the ridge make a left turn for the short finishing climb to Waterrock Knob. There is a visitors center with parking on top with restrooms.

Directions - At the junction of routes 441 and 19 in Cherokee, NC turn north on 19. Head north for several miles through much congestion to the Happy Holidays RV Park (left) where the listed climb begins.

19 North/Waterrock Knob

Total elevation - 2,560 ft	**Length - 8.0 miles**
Average Grade - 6.1% (9%)	**Rating - 1.64 (cat 1)**

Another route to Waterrock Knob heads south on Route 19 for just over 3 fairly steep miles and then you turn left (north) on the Blue Ridge Parkway (see previous climb). A solid grade will work you and there is some traffic on Route 19.

Directions - The climb begins at the north end of the town of Maggie Valley, NC on Route 19. The start is unmarked but you will be able to pick up the grade change.

Cherokee Hill

Total elevation - 3,155 ft	**Length - 10.4 miles**
Average Grade - 5.7% (9%)	**Rating - 1.87 (cat 1)**

The very beginning (or end) of the Blue Ridge Parkway, Cherokee Hill is very scenic and heads through multiple (5) tunnels along its route, ending at an unmarked summit just beyond its fifth tunnel. It is rated the most difficult individual Parkway climb.

Directions - From Cherokee, NC head north on 441 for several miles (toward Great Smoky Mtns National Park). The Blue Ridge Parkway will be on your right and the climb begins just beyond the junction by continuing on the Parkway.

Clingmans Dome East

| Total elevation - 4,261 ft | Length - 22.5 miles |
| Average Grade - 3.6% (8%) | Rating - 1.66 (cat 1) |

The east side of Clingmans Dome is a long and shallow climb up to altitude that carries a lot of traffic. After ~10 miles there is a section of switchback which carries a steeper grade. At mile 15.6 turn left on the road to Clingmans Dome and the listed climb ends at the parking area at the end of the road.

Directions - From Cherokee, NC head north on 441 for several miles (toward Great Smoky Mtns National Park). The climb begins at the Visitors Center by continuing west on 441.

Cherohala Skyway East

| Total elevation - 3,335 ft | Length - 11.6 miles |
| Average Grade - 5.5% (10%) | Rating - 1.87 (cat 1) |

Cherohala Skyway is one of the most scenic and isolated climbs in the U.S. The top is reached after 11.5 miles (small parking area on the right - Huckleberry trailhead). After a descent the road continues to climb intermittently but without significant elevation gain.

Directions - In Robbinsville, NC go west on route 143. In 8/10ths mile turn left on Massey Branch Rd. Stay on Massey Branch for 3.4 miles and then turn right on 143 (Santeetlah Rd). Travel 4.5 miles to the corner of Santeetlah and Blue Boar Rd (right) to begin.

Burkemont Road

Total elevation - 1,160 ft   **Length - 2.7 miles**
Average Grade - 8.1% (11%)   **Rating - 0.94 (cat 2)**

Burkemont Road is a very tough climb up South Mountain just south of Morganton, NC. The first half carries the steepest grade.

Directions - In Morganton, NC head south on Route 64 for 0.7 miles to Salem Road on the left. Travel Salem for 1.1 miles to Burkmont Road. Head down Burkmont Rd for 1.0 miles to begin the listed climb.

Green River Cove Road

Total elevation - 970 ft   **Length - 2.4 miles**
Average Grade - 7.6% (12%)   **Rating - 0.73 (cat 2)**

Green River Cove Road is a quite a challenge as it rises up from the Green River through more switchbacks per mile than any other climb the author as seen. The grade will challenge you as well, particularly through the tight turns. This hill is a very difficult descent.

Directions - In Columbus, NC head west on I-26 to exit 59. Turn right at the top of the exit and then a quick left on Green River Cove Road (top of the climb). Descend (careful) and turn around to begin the climb.

Howard Gap Road

Total elevation - 802 ft   **Length - 1.4 miles**
Average Grade - 10.8% (16%)   **Rating - 0.87 (cat 2)**

Howard Gap Road is included as it contains the steepest mile in NC and perhaps the SE (final mile is 14% grade).

Directions - In Columbus, NC take route 108 south for a very short distance and Howard Gap Road will be on your right (after passing Old Howard Gap Rd). The listed climb begins 1.6 miles up the road.

Saluda Grade

Total elevation - 1,006 ft   **Length - 3.6 miles**
Average Grade - 5.3% (8%)   **Rating - 0.53 (cat 3)**

Saluda Grade is a pleasant and scenic climb with some traffic very close to the SC border. The climb ends at an unmarked top.

Directions - In Tryon, NC at the junction of routes 108 and 276 head west on 276. The listed climb begins 3.2 miles up the road (unmarked).

South Carolina

Ceasars Head

Total elevation - 1,815 ft
Average Grade - 6.1% (9%)

Length - 5.6 miles
Rating - 1.13 (cat 1/2)

The most difficult climb in South Carolina, Ceasars Head (Route 276) is surprisingly tough. The route is twisty and through thick woods. The climb ends at the upper end of the State Park Visitors Center. Take the short walk to perhaps the most scenic overlook in the SE as well.

Directions - From Route 276 where it splits off from Route 11 South continue on 276. Continue for 1.7 miles to Lakemont Rd (left). The listed climb begins 0.2 miles further up 276.

Paris Mountain West

Total elevation - 813 ft
Average Grade - 6.7% (10%)

Length - 2.3 miles
Rating - 0.54 (cat 3)

Used in the US Pro Championships, the climb up the west side of Paris Mountain is a fairly steep and scenic ascent. Near the top houses appear and the summit is unmarked but obvious. The other side of the climb is a rolling ascent from State Park Road.

Directions - On Route 25 South in Travelers Rest, SC take New Roe Ford Road (go left). Almost immediately you turn left at the stop sign (Old Buncombe Rd) and Altamont Rd appears on the right shortly. Head up Altamont Rd to begin the climb.

Tennessee

Stoney Fork Road East

Total elevation - 1,710 ft	**Length - 4.8 miles**
Average Grade - 6.7% (11%)	**Rating - 1.15 (cat 1/2)**

This is a fairly steep and twisty climb into the Smokey Mountains north of Knoxville, TN. The pavement ends on the other side of the climb (stats are estimated).

Directions - From I-75 in tiny Caryville,TN the climb begins by heading west from town on Mountain Rd.

Roan Mountain North

Total elevation - 3,097 ft	**Length - 9.0 miles**
Average Grade - 6.5% (10%)	**Rating - 2.13 (cat 1)**

The north side of Roan Mountain is one of most difficult in the Southeast. Steeper over its bottom half, the road switchbacks up the hill under a tunnel of trees with some good views near the top. At mile 7.5 (Carvers Gap) enter North Carolina and turn right on Roan Mountain Rd for the final 1.5 miles before ending at a tollbooth.

Directions - From the small town of Roan Mountain, TN on route 19E head south on route 143. Travel 143 for 5.5 rolling miles to begin the climb at Burbank Rd (on the left).

107 West

Total elevation - 1,262ft	**Length - 4.1 miles**
Average Grade - 5.8% (9%)	**Rating - 0.75 (cat 2)**

This is a scenic climb to the NC state line.

Directions - From Unicoi, TN head east on 107 to its junction with 173 (left). The listed climb begins just past the junction.

19 West

Total elevation - 1,233 ft	**Length - 5.2 miles**
Average Grade - 4.5% (9%)	**Rating - 0.56 (cat 3)**

One of the most scenic climbs in this guide, 19 West is a very isolated climb through stands of big trees along a variable grade. The first half is the steepest and the grade eases near the NC line, finishing at Spivey Gap in NC.

Directions - From I-26 south of Erwin, TN take exit 12 to 19W. Head down 19W for 3.4 scenic miles to its listed start in Wyatts Branch.

Clingmans Dome West

Total elevation - 4,826 ft	**Length - 20.1 miles**
Average Grade - 4.6% (8%)	**Rating - 2.36 (cat 1)**

Perhaps the most difficult SE climb, the west side of Clingmans

Dome is also a scenic ascent that does carry a lot of traffic. At mile 13 you enter NC and soon after turn right to finish at the parking area for Clingmans Dome.

Directions - In Gatlinburg, TN head east on route 441 for several miles, entering Great Smokey Mountains National Park. The climb begins at the visitor's center (on right).

Cherohala West

Total elevation - 4,346 ft	**Length - 24.2 miles**
Average Grade - 3.4% (10%)	**Rating - 1.53 (cat 1)**

The west side of Cherohala Skyway is a very long and scenic climb along Route 165. The route includes a steep section and there are descents along the way. You enter NC at Beech Gap and continue to climb/descend /climb to an unmarked top. The listed stats are estimates.

Directions - In Tellico Plains, TN head east on 165 for several miles to where the road pulls away from the river to the left. The climb begins shortly after you make the turn.

Lookout Mountain (Rock City)

Total elevation - 957 ft	**Length - 2.9 miles**
Average Grade - 6.3% (10%)	**Rating - 0.60 (cat 2)**

This is the first of 5 routes up Lookout Mountain that begin in TN. The start is steep then the route levels off before a final steep section with great views of the valley to your left. The listed climb ends at Mockingbird Lane with Rock City to your left.

Directions - In Chattanooga, TN head north on Broad St to Route 17. Head south on 17 for a short distance to Ochs Highway on the right (stoplight) to begin the climb.

Ochs Highway

Total elevation - 1,437 ft   **Length - 3.5 miles**
Average Grade - 7.8% (10%)   **Rating - 1.12 (cat 1/2)**

Ochs Highway shares its start with the previous climb. At mile 2.0 turn right to remain on Ochs up a twisty road. At mile 2.8 turn left on Scenic Highway and then right on N Bragg Street. The climb ends at the highpoint of Lookout Mtn at W Averill St (just beyond the water tower on left).

Directions - See previous climb.

Ochs Highway/Sanders Rd/Scenic Highway

Total elevation - 1,425 ft   **Length - 3.7 miles**
Average Grade - 7.3% (11%)   **Rating - 1.04 (cat 1/2)**

From the start of Ochs Highway (previous climb), at mile 1.2 turn right on Sanders Rd. Sanders begins as steep but soon flattens. At mile 1.9 turn left on Scenic Highway along a steeper grade. At East Brow (mile 2.8) turn right and continue to climb through a neighborhood. The listed climb ends at the incline railway (right).

Directions - See previous climb.

Scenic Highway

Total elevation - 1,248 ft   **Length - 3.4 miles**
Average Grade - 7.0% (9%)   **Rating - 0.87 (cat 2)**

Scenic Highway takes you to the top of Lookout Mountain in perhaps the most direct way. At East Brow turn right and continue to climb through a neighborhood. The listed climb ends at the incline railway.

Directions - In Chattanooga, TN head to the junction of Broad St and Highway 11/41. Take 11/41 west for 0.8 miles where the climb begins by heading up Scenic Highway (on your left).

318/Scenic Highway

Total elevation - 1,435 ft   **Length - 4.0 miles**
Average Grade - 6.8% (10%)   **Rating - 0.98 (cat 2)**

Another way up Lookout Mountain, after a steep start the route flattens before it's junction with Scenic Highway. Turn right on Scenic Highway and the route mirrors the previous climb from this point.

Directions - In Chattanooga, TN head to the junction of Broad Street and Highway 11/41. Head west on 11/41 for several miles to Route 318 (on left). Head down 318 for 0.9 miles to Garden Rd on the right where the climb begins by continuing on 318.

Good views on Lookout Mountain, TN

A switchback on TN's Brayton Mountain Rd.

Elder Mountain Road

Total elevation - 1,147 ft   **Length - 2.7 miles**
Average Grade - 8.0% (10%)   **Rating - 0.92 (cat 2)**

Elder Mountain Road is another Chattanooga area short and steep ascent up to a private development. The climb ends at the gate house.

Directions - In Chattanooga, TN head west on I-24 to exit 175. Head north on Browns Ferry Rd and Elder Mountain Road will appear on your left after a short distance. Head up Elder Mountain Rd a short distance to O'Grady Rd (right) where the climb begins.

Raccoon Mountain

Total elevation - 1,063 ft   **Length - 2.7 miles**
Average Grade - 7.5% (9%)   **Rating - 0.79 (cat 2)**

Raccoon Mountain is another solid Chattanooga area climb and shares its start with Elder Mtn Rd (previous climb). After ~1 mile on Elder Mtn Rd turn left toward the pumping station and go left again immediately. The climb ends at an overlook on top of the mountain.

Directions - In Chattanooga, TN head west on I-24 to exit 175. Head north on Browns Ferry Rd and Elder Mountain Road will appear on your left after a short distance. Head up Elder Mountain Rd a short distance to O'Grady Rd (right) where the climb begins.

Signal Mountain

Total elevation - 1,249 ft   **Length - 4.3 miles**
Average Grade - 5.5% (9%)   **Rating - 0.69 (cat 2)**

The main road up Signal Mountain is a pleasant climb but does carry some traffic. A steady grade and views of the Tennessee River near the top make it worthwhile however and the listed climb ends at Rolling Way.

Directions - In Chattanooga, TN head north on Route 27. Exit toward 127 West/Signal Mountain and the listed stats begin at the junction of Mountain Road (right).

W Road

Total elevation - 1,213 ft   **Length - 3.4 miles**
Average Grade - 6.8% (12%)   **Rating - 0.82 (cat 2)**

The cyclists route up Signal Mountain, W Road is a classic climb along a dark road. Near the top a set of stacked switchbacks with the maximum grade on the route brings you to the top of the climb. The listed stats end just before Wilson Rd on the right in Walden on top of the mountain.

Directions - In Chattanooga, TN head north on Route 27. Exit toward 127 West/Signal Mountain for several miles to Mountain Road on the right. Head north on Mountain Rd for a short distance and W Road appears on the left. The climb begins at the junction.

Suck Creek Road

Total elevation - 1,148 ft	**Length - 4.1 miles**
Average Grade - 5.3% (8%)	**Rating - 0.61 (cat 2)**

Suck Creek Road is a bit less steep than most in the area but it is still a pleasant climb with a little bit of traffic. It ends at an unmarked top.

Directions - In Chattanooga, TN head north on Route 27. Exit toward 127 West/Signal Mountain and pass Mountain Road on the right. Just beyond Mountain Road, Suck Creek Road appears on the left. Take Suck Creek Road for several miles and the climb begins when Suck Creek Rd makes a 90 degree turn away from the Tennessee River.

27 West

Total elevation - 1,204 ft	**Length - 4.2 miles**
Average Grade - 5.4% (8%)	**Rating - 0.65 (cat 2)**

This is a pleasant climb up Signal Mountain. A steady grade and nice scenery makes this a good route to the top and is a fun descent.

Directions - At the junction of 283 and 27 in tiny Powells Crossroads, TN (just east of Whitwell) head east on 27 to Smith Cemetery Rd (left) where the climb begins by continuing east on Route 27.

127 West

Total elevation - 1,333 ft   **Length - 4.3 miles**
Average Grade - 5.9% (9%)   **Rating - 0.78 (cat 2)**

Another pleasant climb out of the Sequatchie Valley, the listed stats of 127 West end at Horseshoe Road (left) near the top of the Signal Mountain plateau.

Directions -. At the junction of 127 and 28 just south of Dunlap, TN head east on 127 to its junction with 283 where the climb begins.

Henson Gap Road

Total elevation - 933 ft   **Length - 2.0 miles**
Average Grade - 8.8% (14%)   **Rating - 0.82 (cat 2)**

Henson Gap Road is a great climb along a dark and narrow route that parallels 4 lane 111. Several switchbacks pack double digit grade and the road is lightly travelled. The listed top is unmarked and the road continues to climb after a descent but significant climbing has ended.

Directions - In Dunlap, TN head east on 111 to East Valley Road. Travel East Valley Rd south for a short distance and Henson Gap Rd appears (suddenly) on the left. The listed stats begin 0.5 miles up Henson Gap Rd.

Robert Mills Road

Total elevation - 1,152 ft	**Length - 2.1 miles**
Average Grade - 10.4% (14%)	**Rating - 1.20 (cat 1)**

The route up Robert Mills Road is a difficult and classic climb. Very twisty and dark, it contains multiple hairpin turns with fearsome grade and except for its very beginning and end is steep throughout. Enjoy this one.

Directions - Just south of Soddy-Daisy,TN head west on Robert Mills Rd from Dayton Pike. The listed climb begins at its junction with Selcer Rd on the right.

Montlake Road

Total elevation - 949 ft	**Length - 2.3 miles**
Average Grade - 7.8% (10%)	**Rating - 0.74 (cat 2)**

Montlake Road is a scenic and steep climb up a ridge above Soddy-Daisy, TN. The listed climb ends at Brow Lake Rd on your right.

Directions - From Dayton Pike in Soddy-Daisy, TN take Montlake Road west for 0.9 miles to begin the climb.

Mowbray Road

Total elevation - 924 ft	**Length - 2.5 miles**
Average Grade - 7.0% (10%)	**Rating - 0.65 (cat 2)**

Mowbray Road is another of the multiple short and sweet climbs up the southern Cumberland Plateau. It is steeper over its first half and the listed statistics end after 2.5 miles. Continue a short distance further and the end of Montlake Rd (previous climb) will be on your left.

Directions - From Dayton Pike in Daisy, TN head west on Mowbray Road to begin the climb. As of 11/08 the road was not marked at its intersection with Dayton Pike.

Brayton Mountain Road

Total elevation - 876 ft	**Length - 2.2 miles**
Average Grade - 7.5% (11%)	**Rating - 0.66 (cat 2)**

The climb up Brayton Mountain Rd is a good one through thick woods and along a solid grade. A double switchback near the top will get your attention and the listed climb ends at the Quiet Oaks Assisted Living Home on the right. The road continues to climb intermittently.

Directions - In tiny Graysville, TN head west on Pikeville Ave from Route 303 in the middle of town. 1.7 miles later the road becomes Brayton Mountain Rd and the climb begins at the creek crossing.

Fredonia Road

Total elevation - 1,127 ft	**Length - 2.9 miles**
Average Grade - 7.4% (12%)	**Rating - 0.83 (cat 2)**

Fredonia Road is another enjoyable climb out of Sequatchie Valley in Tennessee. The grade will challenge you and there is excellent hang gliding in the area as well.

Directions - From Route 127 in Dunlap, TN head west on Fredonia Rd for 0.4 miles to Davis Rd (left) to begin the climb.

Daus Mountain Road

Total elevation - 1,220 ft   **Length - 2.8 miles**
Average Grade - 8.3% (17%)   **Rating - 1.03 (cat 1/2)**

A very steep ascent, Daus Mountain Road is a classic climb along a twisty and narrow road. Its first 2 miles average >9% and it contains one of the steepest half miles in the US within its first half. The listed climb ends just shy of Solar Lane on the left.

Directions - In tiny Daus, TN Daus Mountain Rd heads west from West Valley Rd. The climb begins just west of the junction.

108 East

Total elevation - 1,032 ft   **Length - 3.2 miles**
Average Grade - 6.1% (9%)   **Rating - 0.63 (cat 2)**

The east side of 108 is a pleasant climb. Never really steep, the grade will work you however and the road carries a bit of traffic.

Directions - In tiny Whitwell, TN head east on 108 through a 4 way stop intersection. From that intersection the listed climb begins 0.3 miles down 108 at Pine Street on the left.

Sequatchie Mountain Road

Total elevation - 1,049 ft   **Length - 1.8 miles**
Average Grade - 11.0% (13%)   **Rating - 1.16 (cat 1/2)**

One of the steepest ascents in the U.S., Sequatchie Mountain Road is a classic climb. Short and sweet, it is along a fairly steady grade which seems to ease its fearsome average grade (somewhat).

Directions - In miniscule Sequatchie, TN, Sequatchie Mountain Rd takes off from Valley View Rd (main street) and is unmarked. The listed climb begins 0.1 miles down the road.

156 East

Total elevation - 1,039 ft   **Length - 2.1 miles**
Average Grade - 9.4% (12%)   **Rating - 0.97 (cat 2)**

156 East is a steep climb along a heavily wooded ridge near the Alabama border. Light traffic makes this a very pleasant ascent despite the harsh grade.

Directions - From main street in South Pittsburg, TN head east on 156 for 0.6 miles (Birch Ave on left) to begin the climb.

Virginia

33 East (WV border)

Total elevation - 1,416 ft   **Length - 4.1 miles**
Average Grade - 6.5% (9%)   **Rating - 0.93 (cat 2)**

This is a somewhat isolated and pleasant climb within George Washington National Forest to the West Virginia border. A steady and challenging grade will make you work for the top and a bit of traffic will keep you on your toes.

Directions - From Harrisonburg, VA head west on Route 33 for ~ 15 miles to an obvious grade change (dirt Laurel Woods Lane on the right) where the climb begins.

Reddish Knob

Total elevation - 2,635 ft   **Length - 9.1 miles**
Average Grade - 5.5% (10%)   **Rating - 1.64 (cat 1)**

Reddish Knob is a challenging and scenic ascent up to the very top of Reddish Knob Mountain. The road is narrow and the grade is shallow to start but steepens after you pass the dam. Beyond the dam the climb averages ~ 7% grade and at a big switchback at mile 6.8 the road gets very narrow (only one vehicle can pass at a time in places). There are several short flats as you near the top which greets you with 360 degree views. Reddish Knob is also a very fun descent.

Directions - From the small town of Dayton, VA head west on

Route 257. Turn left at the stop sign (stay on 257) and in 2.8 miles turn right to remain on 257. In approximately 3 miles the listed climb begins at the junction with Tilghman Rd on the left by continuing straight.

250 East

Total elevation - 1,267 ft	**Length - 4.4 miles**
Average Grade - 5.4% (8%)	**Rating - 0.69 (cat 2)**

250 West is an isolated and pleasant climb that takes you into West Virginia, A steady grade and nice scenery combine for an enjoyable ride. To warm up it is advised to ride the 2 smaller climbs to get to the start from Monterrey, VA.

Directions - From Monterrey, VA head west on Route 250 for 8.1 miles and over 2 passes. The climb begins at a creek crossing just before Route 600 on the left.

606 East

Total elevation - 1,777 ft	**Length - 4.2 miles**
Average Grade - 8.0% (12%)	**Rating - 1.42 (cat 1)**

The east side of 606 is a real treat. Isolated and unknown to most, the grade is severe over much of the ascent. The first stretch is along a creek and soon the grade steepens as the road switchbacks up the ridge with double digit grade in places.Turn right at mile 4.0 on 713 for 0.2 miles to finish. A classic climb.

Directions - In downtown Clifton Forge, VA head west on Chester to Rose Ave and go north. Rose Ave turns into Sioux

Ave which becomes 606 after crossing under I-64. Head down 606 for 3 miles and the end of a descent to begin the climb.

Wintergreen

Total elevation - 2,664 ft   **Length - 6.1 miles**
Average Grade - 8.3% (13%)   **Rating - 2.30 (cat 1)**

The climb to Wintergreen is likely the most difficult in Virginia. A shallow grade to start, the grade jumps up severely before the turnoff to Wintergreen (to the right) at the 2 mile mark. The grade continues to be double digit after the turnoff and then eases. You turn left at mile 4.6 to continue on Wintergreen Drive with an increase in grade. The grade then eases and at mile 5.4 turn left on Devils Knob Loop Drive. The first section of this road is severe and then the grade eases to finish at an unmarked top just beyond Fern Court on your right.

Directions - From the tiny town of Wintergreen, VA on route 151 head south for a few miles to Route 664. Turn right on 664 and head up the road for 2.6 miles where the listed climb begins at its junction with Falls Rd on the right.

Reeds Gap East

Total elevation - 1,468 ft   **Length - 3.1 miles**
Average Grade - 9.0% (14%)   **Rating - 1.36 (cat 1)**

The climb to Reeds Gap is one of the steepest in the Southeast. An easy start soon turns to terror as over the last mile the grade reaches 12% for sustained stretches. The climb finally ends at the Blue Ridge Parkway.

The turnoff to Wintergreen in Virginia

The top of Virginia's Reeds Gap

Directions - From the tiny town of Wintergreen, VA on route 151 head south on 151 for a few miles to Route 664. Turn right on 664 and head up the road for 2.6 miles where the climb begins at its junction with Falls Rd on the right.

Reeds Gap West

Total elevation - 924 ft	**Length - 2.0 miles**
Average Grade - 8.7% (11%)	**Rating - 0.81 (cat 2)**

The other side climb to Reeds Gap is also one of the steepest in the Southeast along a very scenic route, ending at the Blue Ridge Parkway.

Directions - From Waynesboro, VA head north on route 814 for ~8 miles to 664 on your left. The climb begins by heading up Route 664.

Vesuvius

Total elevation - 1,683 ft	**Length - 4.2 miles**
Average Grade - 7.6% (14%)	**Rating - 1.33 (cat 1)**

One of the most beautiful climbs in the region, Vesuvius is also a difficult ascent. The middle core hits double digit grade in places and the climb ends beyond the Blue Ridge Parkway at an unmarked top. It is a very challenging descent.

Directions - In the tiny town of Vesuvius, VA the climb begins by following the Tye River Parkway after crossing a set of railroad tracks.

56 East

Total elevation - 1,964 ft   **Length - 8.1 miles**
Average Grade - 4.6% (10%)   **Rating - 0.90 (cat 2)**

The other side of Vesuvius, the east side of Route 56 is a variable grade and scenic climb along a narrow road with some steep stretches near the top.

Directions - From the junction of routes 151 and 56 south of tiny Jonesboro, VA head west on 56 for ~8 miles to the North Fork of the Tye River where the climb begins.

Thunder Hill

Total elevation - 3,246 ft   **Length - 12.2 miles**
Average Grade - 5.0% (8%)   **Rating - 1.68 (cat 1)**

One of the most difficult individual hills on the Blue Ridge Parkway and the longest climb in VA, Thunder Hill is a pleasant ascent along a steady grade, ending at an unmarked top.
Directions - From Big Island, VA head west on 501 for a short distance to the Blue Ridge Parkway. The climb begins by heading south on the Parkway.

43 South

Total elevation - 1,336 ft   **Length - 3.0 miles**
Average Grade - 8.4% (10%)   **Rating - 1.13 (cat 1/2)**

Another route to the Blue Ridge Parkway, the south side of 43 carries a steep grade and is a scenic ascent.

Directions - From 221 in Bedford, VA head north on Route 43 for 7.2 miles to begin the listed climb (gift shop on left).

695 South

Total elevation - 1,116 ft	**Length - 2.3 miles**
Average Grade - 9.2% (14%)	**Rating - 1.03 (cat 1/2)**

A surprisingly steep way to reach the Blue Ridge Parkway on a road that sees little traffic. 695 is a very challenging and scenic climb.

Directions - From Route 460 in Montvale, VA head north on 695 (Goose Creek Valley Rd) for 7.6 miles to Craig Lane on the right. The listed climb begins 0.2 miles further up 695.

43 North

Total elevation - 1,409 ft	**Length - 4.1 miles**
Average Grade - 6.5% (9%)	**Rating - 0.92 (cat 2)**

This is a pleasant climb from Buchanon, VA up to the Blue Ridge Parkway. The grade is steady and the route is scenic all the way to the top.

Directions - In Buchanon, VA on I-81 head east on route 43 for 0.7 miles to begin the climb right after you cross beneath a railroad bridge.

Mill Mountain

Total elevation - 775 ft   **Length - 1.9 miles**
Average Grade - 7.7% (11%)   **Rating - 0.60 (cat 2)**

Mill Mountain is a good town climb in Roanoke Virginia. After 0.3 miles turn right on Sylvan and then left to head up the mountain. Multiple switchbacks make this an enjoyable climb. You can also go straight at the junction with Sylvan (2.7 miles at 5.4%)

Directions - In Roanoke, VA take Walnut Avenue east from Highway 220. The climb begins at Bellview Avenue (on the right) a short distance down Walnut Avenue.

311 South (WV border)

Total elevation - 1,134 ft   **Length - 3.4 miles**
Average Grade - 6.3% (9%)   **Rating - 0.72 (cat 2)**

This is a pleasant climb up Reeds Mountain along a steady and solid grade. The summit is signed and ends at the WV border.

Directions - The climb begins at the junction of 311 and route 18 in tiny Paint Blank, VA by continuing north on 311.

311 North

Total elevation - 1,619 ft   **Length - 5.5 miles**
Average Grade - 5.6% (8%)   **Rating - 0.90 (cat 2)**

311 North is a nice climb up to an unmarked summit. Little traffic and a solid grade make for a pleasant ascent.

Directions - The climb begins in Paint Blank, VA at the junction with Route 600 by continuing south on 311.

311 South

Total elevation - 1,750 ft	Length - 4.8 miles
Average Grade - 6.9% (9%)	Rating - 1.21 (cat 1)

The south side of 311 is a stout test along a heavily wooded ridge. The grade is fairly steady and there are several switchbacks to help you to the top.

Directions - From New Castle, VA head north on Route 311 for ~5 miles to route 658 on your left. Go beyond 658 for a short distance and the listed climb begins at the end of a descent.

Mountain Lake

Total elevation - 2,115 ft	Length - 6.4 miles
Average Grade - 6.3% (10%)	Rating - 1.35 (cat 1)

Used in the now defunct Tour DuPont (Lance Armstrong won a stage on its slopes) Mountain Lake is a difficult climb along a very scenic route. There is a lodge and cabins at the top.

Directions - From Blacksburg, VA head west on Route 460 beyond the small town of Newport for several miles to Route 700 on the right. The climb begins at the dip in the creek bed just after you turn onto Route 700 (Mountain Lake Rd).

613 (Doe Creek Road)

Total elevation - 1,895 ft	Length - 4.2 miles
Average Grade - 8.6% (13%)	Rating - 1.62 (cat 1)

The more difficult ascent to Mountain Lake, 613 (Doe Creek Rd) is steeper, perhaps more scenic and one of the most difficult climbs in the SE. The first half is a good warmup but the majority of the last 1.5 miles is along double digit grade and will hurt you. The previous climb, Mountain Lake, is an easier descent.

Directions - From Blacksburg, VA head west on Route 460 to the small town of Newport. Continue west on 460 for ~5 miles to route 613 (Doe Creek Rd) on your right. Head up Route 613 for 0.8 miles where the climb begins just after a small descent (unmarked start).

Little Walker Mountain South

Total elevation - 658 ft	Length - 1.7 miles
Average Grade - 7.3% (10%)	Rating - 0.48 (cat 3)

A short but sweet climb along a very narrow road in Southwest Virginia, Little Walker South is worth the effort to get to its isolated start.

Directions - From Pulaski, VA head west on Robinson Tract Rd which becomes route 738. The climb begins where the grade increases just beyond the tiny community of Weldon.

Little Walker Mountain North

Total elevation - 692 ft	**Length - 2.2 miles**
Average Grade - 6.0% (8%)	**Rating - 0.41 (cat 3)**

The other side of Little Walker Mountain is a bit longer and less steep (and less scenic).

Directions - West of Pulaski, VA, the climb begins at the junction of routes 600 and 738 by heading east on 738.

Walker Mountain South

Total elevation - 1,129 ft	**Length - 3.3 miles**
Average Grade - 6.5% (10%)	**Rating - 0.73 (cat 2)**

This is a great and isolated climb along the most narrow road the author has seen that allows auto traffic. The 2nd half contains stacked switchbacks and a grade that will challenge you.

Directions - West of Pulaski, VA, the climb begins at the junction of routes 600 and 738 by heading west on 738.

Walker Mountain North

Total elevation - 703 ft	**Length - 3.3 miles**
Average Grade - 4.0% (8%)	**Rating - 0.28 (cat 3)**

The other side of Walker Mountain, while identical in length, is a more shallow climb along a scenic route.

Directions - In Mechanicsburg, VA head east on Route 738 for several miles to route 670 (left) where the listed climb begins.

Squirrel Spur Road

Total elevation - 1,151ft	**Length - 2.9 miles**
Average Grade - 7.5% (9%)	**Rating - 0.87 (cat 2)**

The first of 5 parallel climbs in fairly close proximity, Squirrel Spur Rd may be the easiest of the bunch. It carries a steady grade and little traffic and ends at an unmarked top 0.8 miles shy of the Blue Ridge Parkway.

Directions - In Mt Airy, NC head north on 103 from Highway 52. Still in town take Route 104 toward the VA line. After crossing into VA the road becomes Ararat Highway. Follow this for several miles to Squirrel Spur Rd. Turn left on Squirrel Spur and the listed climb begins in 0.6 miles (unmarked).

Willis Gap

Total elevation - 1,223 ft	**Length - 2.6 miles**
Average Grade - 8.9% (11%)	**Rating - 1.09 (cat 1/2)**

The climb to Willis Gap is a difficult ride up to the Blue Ridge Parkway. One of the steepest grades in the SE, it is at least fairly uniform much of the way. Light traffic makes this a pleasant route with opportunities to make climbing loops with other nearby ascents.

Directions - In Mt Airy, NC head north on 103 from Route 52.

Still in town take Route 104 (left) toward the VA line. Just before the state line, Willis Gap Road appears on your left. The listed climb begins several miles up Willis Gap Rd at its junction with Valley End Rd on the right.

Orchard Gap

Total elevation - 983 ft	**Length - 2.2 miles**
Average Grade - 8.5% (15%)	**Rating - 0.80 (cat 2)**

Orchard Gap may be the most dramatic of the area climbs. Short and sweet, it contains a double switchback that you will remember (20% grade inside corner with double digit grade after the 2nd switchback). It is a great way to reach the Parkway.

Directions - From Cana, VA on Highway 52 turn right on Route 686. In 2.8 miles turn left on Wards Gap Rd. Take Wards Gap Rd for 3.6 miles to an intersection. Continue straight (the road becomes Orchard Gap Rd) and the listed climb begins at Willow Hill Rd on the right in 0.8 miles.

52 South

Total elevation - 1,391 ft	**Length - 4.5 miles**
Average Grade - 5.9% (9%)	**Rating - 0.82 (cat 2)**

Route 52 is a solid climb up to the Blue Ridge Parkway. There are some steep sections, narrow shoulders and a lot of traffic to keep you on your toes. This is the least attractive route in the area up to the Parkway.

Directions - From the state line between NC and VA on Highway 52 in Cana, VA head north on 52 for 3.7 miles to Route 892 (left) to begin the listed climb.

Pipers Gap

Total elevation - 1,165 ft   **Length - 2.9 miles**

Average Grade - 7.6% (16%)   **Rating - 0.92 (cat 2)**

Pipers Gap is a superb climb up a heavily forested ridge to the Blue Ridge Parkway. European like (wide single lane), its lower and middle sections contain double digit grade and will test you but a very scenic route will help ease the pain. The grade eases over its last mile and the climb ends under the Parkway. This is a must do climb.

Directions - From tiny Lambsburg, VA off of I-77 just north of the North Carolina state line, head west on Lambsburg Road (Route 620) to begin the climb in town at its junction with Route 944 on the right.

58/Grayson Highlands

Total elevation - 1,743 ft   **Length - 7.2 miles**

Average Grade - 4.6% (9%)   **Rating - 0.80 (cat 2)**

After a steep start the grade flattens out as you approach Grayson Highlands State Park. Turn right into the park along a very scenic and shallow route that ends at a parking area. There is good hiking routes along the way.

Directions - From tiny Volney, VA head west on Route 58 for 5.6 miles to where the climb begins by continuing on 58 as the grade increases dramatically (unmarked start).

Whitetop Road South

Total elevation - 695 ft	**Length - 1.7 miles**
Average Grade - 7.7% (9%)	**Rating - 0.54 (cat 3)**

The south side of Whitetop (Route 600) is a short and steep climb on the flanks of Mt Rogers. It ends as it flattens out near the top of the ridge.

Directions - From the entrance to Grayson Highlands State Park on Route 58 south of Mt Rodgers, head west on Route 58 for ~8 miles to Whitetop Road (on the right) where the listed climb begins.

Whitetop Road North

Total elevation - 1,311 ft	**Length - 4.7 miles**
Average Grade - 5.3% (7%)	**Rating - 0.69 (cat 2)**

Less steep then its south side, the north side of Whitetop Road is a pleasant and scenic climb along a steady grade, ending (unmarked) 0.5 miles north of the county line.

Directions - Just northwest of Mt Rodgers in SW VA the climb begins at the junction of state roads 603 and 600 (Route 600 is also Whitetop Road).

The climb of Virginia's Orchard Gap

Single lane on Virginia's Pipers Gap

52 South

Total elevation - 1,140 ft   **Length - 4.0 miles**
Average Grade - 5.4% (8%)   **Rating - 0.62 (cat 2)**

This is a nice climb close to I-77 that ends at a country store on top.

Directions - From Wytheville, VA head west on 52 for several miles to its junction with Route 717 (right) where the climb begins.

52 North

Total elevation - 843 ft   **Length - 3.5 miles**
Average Grade - 4.6% (8%)   **Rating - 0.38 (cat 3)**

Route 52 North is a pleasant climb along a steady grade that ends at a country store with views.

Directions - From the junction of I-77 and I-81 head north on I-77 for several miles to Route 42/52. Head south and Routes 42 and 52 split in a few miles. Stay south on 52 and the climb begins soon after the split.

Big Mountain Road

Total elevation - 619 ft   **Length - 2.4 miles**
Average Grade - 4.9% (8%)   **Rating - 0.30 (cat 3)**

Big Mountain Rd is a must do climb along a single lane road through very scenic southwestern VA. Never very steep its charm is what you will remember. It ends at the top of the previous climb (Route 52) and can be used to link several other climbs on a loop ride.

Directions - From the junction of Interstates 77 and 81 head north on I-77 for several miles to Route 42/52. Head south and stay on 42 when 52 splits off. Big Mtn Road appears on the left shortly and the listed climb begins 0.5 miles down Big Mountain Road.

16 South

Total elevation - 1,231 ft	**Length - 3.5 miles**
Average Grade - 6.7% (9%)	**Rating - 0.83 (cat 2)**

16 South is an interesting and scenic climb near Interstate 81. Heavily wooded and twisty, it ends at an unmarked summit.

Directions - From I-81 in Marion, VA take Route 16 north for a short distance to Hungry Mother State Park. The climb begins just beyond the lake.

16 North

Total elevation - 1,255 ft	**Length - 3.3 miles**
Average Grade - 7.2% (9%)	**Rating - 0.92 (cat 2)**

The north side of Route 16 is a very solid and isolated climb up to an unmarked summit. The grade will work you on this one and just a little bit of traffic will keep you on your toes.

Directions - See previous climb. The listed stats for 16 North begin at the junction of routes 16 and 610.

High Knob

Total elevation - 1,577 ft	**Length - 3.0 miles**
Average Grade - 10.0% (14%)	**Rating - 1.63 (cat 1)**

High Knob is among the steepest climbs in the Southeast. The first 2 miles are the most difficult and a very narrow road gets you to its unmarked top. Several tight switchbacks will get your undivided attention but very little traffic makes this a great climb. Due to its steep grade it is a very difficult descent.

Directions - From Route 23 in Wise, Virginia exit to route 619. Head south on Route 619 for 0.2 miles where the listed climb begins.

160 East

Total elevation - 1,657 ft	**Length - 4.4 miles**
Average Grade - 7.1% (9%)	**Rating - 1.18 (cat 1)**

The east side of 160 is a great climb up Black Mountain and into KY. The grade is steady and will challenge you all the way up. A little traffic will keep you alert.

Directions - In Appalachia, VA head west on Route 160. Continue right on 160 at its junction with 168 for 3.4 miles to a creek crossing where the listed climb begins.

West Virginia

33 West (VA border)

Total elevation - 1,768 ft   **Length - 5.5 miles**
Average Grade - 6.1% (9%)   **Rating - 1.08 (cat 1/2)**

The west side of Route 33 takes riders to the Virginia border through thick woods and along a challenging route. Several big switchbacks contain the steepest grades on the climb and produce some good views. The grade eases just before the summit. A few big rigs may pass you on this one but it is a worthwhile ascent.

Directions - From tiny Brandywine, WV head east on Route 33 for several miles to Lady Bug Lane on the left where the listed climb begins.

33 West

Total elevation - 1,426 ft   **Length - 5.3 miles**
Average Grade - 5.1% (8%)   **Rating - 0.73 (cat 2)**

Located further west than the previous climb, this west side of Route 33 is a pleasant climb with some traffic. Statistics are estimated on this climb.

Directions - From tiny Judy Gap, WV at the junction of routes 28 and 33, head east on Route 33 for several miles to begin the climb.

15 East

Total elevation - 1,531 ft	**Length - 5.6 miles**
Average Grade - 5.2% (9%)	**Rating - 0.81 (cat 2)**

15 East is a scenic climb away from Route 219 along a narrow road that carries some traffic. It is a pleasant climb however and the listed stats are estimates.

Directions - From Mingo, WV on Route 219 head north on 219 for several miles. Route 15 will be on your left and the climb begins at the junction.

Snowshoe East

Total elevation - 1,503 ft	**Length - 4.4 miles**
Average Grade - 6.5% (13%)	**Rating - 1.00 (cat 1/2)**

The east side approach to the Snowshoe Ski area is a Jekyll and Hyde climb. The first few miles along 66 (a little traffic) are a solid climb and then the grade flattens as you turn left on Snowshoe Road. After a continuation of shallow/flat riding the grade rears up and you must negotiate one of the steepest miles in the Southeast to get to its unmarked top. This is a challenging climb to high altitude.

Directions - From the junction of routes 219 and 66 north of Slatyfork, WV head east on 66, passing the first entrance for Snowshoe. The climb begins where the grade increases as you begin to climb the ridge.

Snowshoe West

Total elevation - 1,554 ft   **Length - 4.9 miles**
Average Grade - 6.0% (9%)   **Rating - 0.93 (cat 2)**

The more uniform approach to the Snowshoe Resort, the west side climb is steady and scenic and carries more traffic. The climb ends as the grade levels out at the Shamrock condos on the left.

Directions - From the junction of routes 219 and 66 north of Slatyfork, WV head east on 66 for a short distance. Turn left on the road to Snowshoe and the listed climb begins in 0.8 miles at a creek crossing.

219/150

Total elevation - 2,117 ft   **Length - 9.2 miles**
Average Grade - 4.5% (8%)   **Rating - 0.98 (cat 2)**

219/150 is a long climb up toward Spruce Knob. Beginning in Marlinton the route is variable until you pass the tiny community of Edray where the grade increases as you head up the ridge. Traffic is present on 219. At mile 5.6 turn left on Route 150. The grade and traffic ease as you ascend this scenic route. The listed climb ends at an overlook 1.4 miles before you reach the Spruce Knob Trailhead.

Directions - In Marlinton, WV the climb begins at Spruce Creek Road (left) by heading north on 219.

39/150

Total elevation - 1,657 ft	Length - 5.7 miles
Average Grade - 5.6% (9%)	Rating - 0.93 (cat 2)

39/150 is a pleasant climb through central WV. At mile 3.3 turn right on 150 and climb for another 2.4 miles along a very scenic road to an unmarked top. Route 150 is a Blue Ridge Parkway like roadway and a great rolling ride if taken all the way to Route 219.

Directions - At the junction of 219 and 39 south of Marlinton, WV head west on 39 for several miles to the small community of Stamping Creek. The listed climb begins from Raintown Rd on your left.

Kenneson Mountain

Total elevation - 1,413 ft	Length - 5.2 miles
Average Grade - 5.2% (8%)	Rating - 0.74 (cat 2)

Sharing its start with the previous climb, continue on 39 past its junction with 150 along a steady grade to finish at the signed summit. This is a very scenic area in West Virginia with good hiking possibilities.

Directions - At the junction of 219 and 39 south of Marlinton, WV head west on 39 for several miles to the small community of Stamping Creek. The listed climb begins from Raintown Rd on your left.

311 North

Total elevation - 973 ft   **Length - 3.1 miles**
Average Grade - 5.9% (8%)   **Rating - 0.58 (cat 2)**

311 North is a short but solid climb up Reeds Mountain to the VA border along a steady grade. Little traffic and nice scenery make for a pleasant ascent.

Directions - The climb begins at the junction of 311 and Route 3 in tiny Sweet Springs, WV near the Virginia border.

West Virginia's Route 33 West

Organized Races/Rides with Significant Climbing

Blood, Sweat and Gears (NC) - > 13,000 feet of climbing over 100 miles through the mountains of northern North Carolina. For details go to www.bloodsweatandgears.org.

Brasstown Bald Buster Century (GA) - > 12,000 feet of climbing over 100 miles through north Georgia and some of the same terrain that the annual Tour de Georgia covers. For details go to www.brasstownbaldbustercentury.com.

Three Mountain Metric (NC) - 8,600 feet of climbing over 75 miles in North Carolina including the very tough climb up Pilot Mountain. Details at www.home.triad.rr.com/threemtnmetric/.

The Blue Ridge Extreme (VA)– A tough 11,141 feet of climbing over 100 miles within the scenic Blue Ridge Mountains. For details go to www.blueridgeextreme.com.

Assault on Mount Mitchell (SC/NC) - 11,000 ft of climbing over 100 miles that ends at the top of Mount Mitchell. For details go to www.freewheelers.info/assaultl.html.

Six Gap Century (GA) - 10,700 ft of climbing over 100 miles through north Georgia. For details go to www.dahlonega.org/sixgapcentury/index.html.

Tour de Cashiers (NC) - 10,500 of climbing over 101 miles through scenic western North Carolina. For details go to www.tourdecashiers.com.

The Mountain Mama Road Bike Challenge (VA) - 10,000 feet of climbing over 100 miles through the scenic but tough Allegheny Mountains of Virginia. For details go to: http://bikemountainmama.homestead.com.

3 State 3 Mountain Challenge (TN) – A unique ride that hits climbs in 3 states (Georgia, Alabama, Tennessee). For details go to: http://chattbike.com/events/3_state/3st100.htm.

The Hot Doggett 100 (NC) – A very scenic ride with climbing near Asheville, NC that includes the tough Doggett Pass. For details go to: http://www.mhc.edu/hotdoggett/

Cheat Mountain Challenge (WV) – 100 miles through the high country of West Virginia. For details go to: www.wvcf.org/CMC/index.html.

Cheaha Century Challenge (AL) – A challenging ride through NE Alabama. For details: http://www.cheahachallenge.com.

Assault on the Carolinas (NC/SC) – A metric century that climbs formidable Ceasars Head. For details go to: http://assaultonthecarolinas.com/ride.html.

Roan Moan (NC/TN) – A scenic and tough ride that uses multiple climbs in this guide including Roan Mountain. For details go to: http://www.bicycleinn.com/RoanMoanInfo05.htm.

50 Most Difficult SE Climbs
(Author Rating; Major Tour Rating)

1.	Clingmans Dome West, TN	(2.34; cat 1)
2.	Wintergreen, VA	(2.30; cat 1)
3.	Brasstown Bald, GA	(2.24; cat 1)
4.	Mt Mitchell, NC	(2.24; cat 1)
5.	Roan Mountain North, TN	(2.13; cat 1)
6.	Roan Mountain South, NC	(2.12; cat 1)
7.	19 South/Waterrock Knob, NC	(2.03; cat 1)
8.	Cherohala Skyway East, NC	(1.87; cat 1)
9.	Cherokee Hill, NC	(1.87; cat 1)
10.	151/Mount Pisgah, NC	(1.75; cat 1)
11.	Thunder Hill, VA	(1.68; cat 1)
12.	Beech Mountain, NC	(1.66; cat 1)
13.	613, VA	(1.65; cat 1)
14.	Clingmans Dome East, NC	(1.65; cat 1)
15.	Reddish Knob, VA	(1.64; cat 1)
16.	19 North/Waterrock Knob, NC	(1.64; cat 1)
17.	High Knob, VA	(1.65; cat 1)
18.	Cherohala Skyway West, TN	(1.53; cat 1)
19.	215 South, NC	(1.50; cat 1)
20.	606 East, VA	(1.45; cat 1)
21.	Hogpen Gap West, GA	(1.39; cat 1)
22.	Reeds Gap East, VA	(1.36; cat 1)
23.	Mountain Lake, VA	(1.35; cat 1)
24.	Vesuvious, VA	(1.33; cat 1)
25.	Waterrock Knob East, NC	(1.29; cat 1)

Most Difficult Climbs Continued:

26.	Doggett Gap East, NC	(1.24; cat 1)
27.	Seven Devils, NC	(1.24; cat 1)
28.	311 South, VA	(1.23; cat 1)
29.	Robert Mills Road, TN	(1.23; cat 1)
30.	Hawksnest, NC	(1.21; cat 1)
31.	Richland Balsam, NC	(1.21; cat 1)
32.	160 East, VA	(1.20; cat 1)
33.	Sequatchie Mountain Road, TN	(1.16; cat 1/2)
34.	Mt Pisgah, NC	(1.16; cat 1/2)
35.	Stoney Fork Road East, TN	(1.15; cat 1/2)
36.	215 North, NC	(1.13; cat 1/2)
37.	Ceasars Head, SC	(1.13; cat 1/2)
38.	Ochs Highway, TN	(1.12; cat 1/2)
39.	Fort Mountain West, GA	(1.11; cat 1/2)
40.	18, NC	(1.10; cat 1/2)
41.	Willis Gap, VA	(1.10; cat 1/2)
42.	16, NC	(1.10; cat 1/2)
43.	33 West, WV	(1.09; cat 1/2)
44.	181, NC	(1.09; cat 1/2)
45.	Mt Jefferson, NC	(1.08; cat 1/2)
46.	Craggy Gardens, NC	(1.07; cat 1/2)
47.	Ochs/Sanders/Scenic Hw, TN	(1.04; cat 1/2)
48.	Daus Mountain Road, TN	(1.03; cat 1/2)
49.	695, VA	(1.03; cat 1/2)
50.	Snowshoe East, WV	(1.02; cat 1/2)

Additional Climbing Categories

Steepest Climbs (min 2.0 miles)

1. Brasstown Bald, GA - 11.1%
2. Hogpen Gap West, GA - 10.7%
3. Robert Mills Road, TN - 10.4%
4. High Knob, VA - 10.0%
5. 156 East, TN - 9.4%
6. Beech Mountain, NC - 9.2%
7. 695, VA - 9.2%
8. Reeds Gap East, VA - 9.0%
9. Willis Gap, VA - 8.9%
10. Pilot Mountain, NC - 8.8%

Greatest Elevation Gain Climbs

1. Mount Mitchell, NC - 5,161 ft
2. Clingmans Dome West, TN - 4,826 ft
3. Cherohala Skyway West, TN - 4,346 ft
4. Clingmans Dome East, NC - 4,261 ft
5. 19 South/Waterrock Knob, NC - 3,580 ft
6. Cherohala Skyway, NC - 3,335 ft
7. Thunder Hill, VA - 3,246 ft
8. Cherokee Hill, NC - 3,155 ft
9. Roan Mountain North, TN - 3,097 ft
10. Craggy Gardens, NC - 2,978 ft

Highest Elevation Attained Climbs

1. Mount Mitchell, NC - 6,586 ft
2. Clingmans Dome, NC/TN - 6,311 ft
3. Roan Mountain, NC - 6,101 ft
4. Richland Balsam, NC - 6,040 ft
5. 19/Waterrock Knob, NC - 5,772 ft
6. Cherohala Skyway West, TN - 5,402 ft
7. 215, NC - 5,343 ft
8. Cherohala Skyway East, NC - 5,300 ft
9. Beech Mountain, NC - 5,285 ft
10. Craggy Gardens, NC - 5,158 ft

Most Technical Descents

1. High Knob, VA
2. Green Cove Road, NC
3. Robert Mills Road, TN
4. Brasstown Bald, GA
5. Seven Devils, NC
6. Henson Gap Road, TN
7. Beech Mountain, NC
8. Vesuvius, VA
9. 156 East, TN
10. Pilot Mountain, NC

Longest Climbs

1. Mount Mitchell, NC - 24.4 miles
2. Cherohala Skyway West, TN - 24.2 miles
3. Clingmans Dome East, NC - 22.5 miles
4. Clingmans Dome West, TN - 20.1 miles
5. Craggy Gardens, NC - 16.2 miles
6. Mount Pisgah, NC - 14.3 miles
7. 19 South/Waterrock Knob, NC - 12.6 miles
8. 181, NC - 12.6 miles
9. Thunder Hill, VA - 12.2 miles
10. Richland Balsam, NC - 11.7 miles

Most Scenic/Spectacular Climbs

1. Cherohala Skyway East, NC
2. Pipers Gap, VA
3. Walker Mountain South, VA
4. 151/Mount Pisgah, NC
5. Lookout Mountain (Rock City), TN
6. Vesuvius, VA
7. Waterrock Knob East, NC
8. Green Cove Road, NC
9. Chimney Peak, AL
10. 19 West, TN

Additional Climbing Resources

Books:

Ascent, The Mountains of the Tour de France by Richard
Yates, Cycle Publishing.
Cycling Colorado's Mountain Passes by Kurt Magsamen,
Fulcrum Publishing, Golden, CO.
Kings of the Mountains by Matt Rendell, Arum Press. London,
England.
The Complete Guide to Climbing (By Bike) by John
Summeson, Extreme Press.
Uphill Battle by Owen Mulholland, Velopress, Boulder, CO.

Magazines:

Bicycling
Cycle Sport America
Pro Cycling
Road
Road Bike Action
Velonews

Selected websites:

Azcycling.com
Bicyling.com
Bikeradar.com
Cyclingnews.com
Dailypeloton.com
Missingsaddle.com
Northeastcycling.com
Roadcycling.com

Spokepost.com
Steephill.tv
Truesport.com
Usacycling.org
Usacyclingclimbing.com
Utahcycling.com
Velonews.com
Westernwheelers.org

Training:

AthletiCamps.com
Bicyclecoach.com
Bikecamp.com
Carmichael Training Systems (trainright.com)
Cycle-Smart.com
Cyclist Training Bible by Joe Friel, Velopress, Boulder, CO.
Eddie B. Cycling World Fitness (Eddiebcyclingworld.com)
EliteFITcoach.com
Tecknowlogysource.com
Peakscoachinggroup.com
Trainingpeaks.com

Forums:

Bicycle.com
BikeForums.net
Bikeradar.com
CyclingForums.com
Dailypeloton.com
Forums.roadbikereview.com
Tinmtn.org - (Mount Washington Hill Climb Forum)
Sports.yahoo.com
Velonews.com

Touring:

Adventure Cycling Association (aventurecycling.org)
Breaking Away Bicycle Tours (breakingaway.com)
Carpenter/Phinney Bike Camp (bikecamp.com)
Cycle America (cycleamerica.com)
Cycle Tours of Italy (cycleitalia.com)
Timberline Adventures (timbertours.com)
Trek Travel Cycling Vacations (trektravel.com)
Velo Classic Tours (veloclassictours.com)

Events:

Active.com
Azcycling.com
Bikereg.com
Bikeride.com
Cycleidaho.com
Montanacycling.org
Northeastcycling.com
Nmcycling.com
Utahcycling.com

Additional Climbs Data Keys

Traffic:

1 – Almost nonexistent traffic
2 – Some traffic, mostly local
3 – Moderate to heavy traffic

Descent:

1 – Fast and smooth
2 – Fast with a few obstacles
3 – Speed somewhat blunted by obstacles (turns, traffic, etc)
4 – Difficult due to road and/or traffic conditions
5 – Danger of bodily harm at almost any speed

The road to Pipers Gap in Virginia

Southeast Climbs Additional Data

Alabama

Mount Cheaha East

Total elevation:	1,407 ft	Length:	4.1 mi
Top elevation:	2,407 ft	Average grade:	6.5%
Minimum grade:	1%	Maximum grade:	11%
Distance > 5%:	2.6 miles	Distance > 10%:	0.1 mi
Steepest mile:	6.9%	Steepest 3 miles:	6.7%
Traffic:	2	Descent:	3

Mount Cheaha West

Total elevation:	1,232 ft	Length:	3.3 mi
Top elevation:	2,407 ft	Average grade:	7.1%
Minimum grade:	3%	Maximum grade:	11%
Distance > 5%:	2.7 miles	Distance > 10%:	0.1 mi
Steepest mile:	7.5%	Steepest 3 miles:	7.2%
Traffic:	1	Descent:	3

Chimney Peak

Total elevation:	891ft	Length:	1.8 mi
Top elevation:	1,694 ft	Average grade:	9.4%
Minimum grade:	0%	Maximum grade:	20%
Distance > 5%:	1.5 miles	Distance > 10%:	0.8mi
Steepest mile:	9.6%	Steepest 3 miles:	NA
Traffic:	1	Descent:	4

__Georgia__

28 South

Total elevation:	2,101 ft	Length:	10.6 mi
Top elevation:	3,771 ft	Average grade:	3.8%
Minimum grade:	0%	Maximum grade:	8%
Distance > 5%:	2.9 miles	Distance > 10%:	0.0 mi
Steepest mile:	5.9%	Steepest 3 miles:	5.5%
Traffic:	1	Descent:	3

246/106

Total elevation:	888 ft	Length:	2.0 mi
Top elevation:	6,264 ft	Average grade:	8.4%
Minimum grade:	5%	Maximum grade:	10%
Distance > 5%:	1.9 miles	Distance > 10%:	0.1 mi
Steepest mile:	8.6%	Steepest 3 miles:	NA
Traffic:	3	Descent:	2

Brasstown Bald

Total elevation:	1,824 ft	Length:	3.1 mi
Top elevation:	4,775 ft	Average grade:	11.1%
Minimum grade:	1%	Maximum grade:	21%
Distance > 5%:	2.9 miles	Distance > 10%:	1.9 mi
Steepest mile:	11.9%	Steepest 3 miles:	11.1%
Traffic:	2	Descent:	4

Hogpen Gap East

Total elevation:	1,247 ft	Length:	2.2 mi
Top elevation:	3,485 ft	Average grade:	10.7%
Minimum grade:	4%	Maximum grade:	13%
Distance > 5%:	2.1 miles	Distance > 10%:	1.2 mi
Steepest mile:	11.3%	Steepest 3 miles:	NA
Traffic:	1	Descent:	2

Hogpen Gap West

Total elevation:	1,431 ft	Length:	4.1 mi
Top elevation:	3,485 ft	Average grade:	6.6%
Minimum grade:	4%	Maximum grade:	9%
Distance > 5%:	3.4 miles	Distance > 10%:	0.0 mi
Steepest mile:	6.9%	Steepest 3 miles:	6.7%
Traffic:	1	Descent:	3

Wolfpen Gap North

Total elevation:	1,054 ft	Length:	3.3 mi
Top elevation:	3,260 ft	Average grade:	6.1%
Minimum grade:	3%	Maximum grade:	10%
Distance > 5%:	2.9 miles	Distance > 10%:	0.0 mi
Steepest mile:	6.6%	Steepest 3 miles:	6.2%
Traffic:	1	Descent:	3

Wolfpen Gap South

Total elevation:	485 ft	Length:	2.1 mi
Top elevation:	3,260 ft	Average grade:	4.4%
Minimum grade:	3%	Maximum grade:	8%
Distance > 5%:	1.0 miles	Distance > 10%:	0.0 mi
Steepest mile:	5.3%	Steepest 3 miles:	NA
Traffic:	1	Descent:	3

Neels Gap East – lack of data

Neels Gap West

Total elevation:	1,101 ft	Length:	5.5 mi
Top elevation:	3,086 ft	Average grade:	3.8%
Minimum grade:	3%	Maximum grade:	9%
Distance > 5%:	3.3 miles	Distance > 10%:	0.0 mi
Steepest mile:	5.8%	Steepest 3 miles:	5.1%
Traffic:	2	Descent:	3

Woody Gap East

Total elevation:	1,281 ft	Length:	5.4 mi
Top elevation:	3,186 ft	Average grade:	4.5%
Minimum grade:	3%	Maximum grade:	8%
Distance > 5%:	2.1 miles	Distance > 10%:	0.0 mi
Steepest mile:	5.6%	Steepest 3 miles:	5.1%
Traffic:	2	Descent:	2

Fort Mountain East

Total elevation:	1,394 ft	Length:	6.4 mi
Top elevation:	2,794 ft	Average grade:	4.1%
Minimum grade:	1%	Maximum grade:	8%
Distance > 5%:	2.2 miles	Distance > 10%:	0.0 mi
Steepest mile:	5.9%	Steepest 3 miles:	5.2%
Traffic:	1	Descent:	2

Fort Mountain West

Total elevation:	1,894 ft	Length:	6.1 mi
Top elevation:	2,664 ft	Average grade:	5.9%
Minimum grade:	0%	Maximum grade:	8%
Distance > 5%:	3.8 miles	Distance > 10%:	0.0 mi
Steepest mile:	6.4%	Steepest 3 miles:	6.2%
Traffic:	1	Descent:	2

Dougherty Gap

Total elevation:	626 ft	Length:	1.6 mi
Top elevation:	1,790 ft	Average grade:	7.4%
Minimum grade:	3%	Maximum grade:	14%
Distance > 5%:	1.5 miles	Distance > 10%:	0.3 mi
Steepest mile:	8.5%	Steepest 3 miles:	NA
Traffic:	1	Descent:	4

136 East

Total elevation:	969 ft	Length:	3.1 mi
Top elevation:	1,996 ft	Average grade:	5.9%
Minimum grade:	3%	Maximum grade:	9%
Distance > 5%:	2.6 miles	Distance > 10%:	0.0 mi
Steepest mile:	6.6%	Steepest 3 miles:	5.9%
Traffic:	2	Descent:	3

Nick A Jack Road

Total elevation:	714 ft	Length:	1.6 mi
Top elevation:	1,502 ft	Average grade:	8.4%
Minimum grade:	4%	Maximum grade:	10%
Distance > 5%:	1.5 miles	Distance > 10%:	0.0 mi
Steepest mile:	8.7%	Steepest 3 miles:	NA
Traffic:	1	Descent:	3

136 West

Total elevation:	1,248 ft	Length:	4.2 mi
Top elevation:	1,984 ft	Average grade:	5.6%
Minimum grade:	3%	Maximum grade:	9%
Distance > 5%:	2.8 miles	Distance > 10%:	0.0 mi
Steepest mile:	6.5%	Steepest 3 miles:	5.8%
Traffic:	2	Descent:	3

Burkhalter Gap

Total elevation:	1,149 ft	Length:	2.6 mi
Top elevation:	1,858 ft	Average grade:	8.4%
Minimum grade:	4%	Maximum grade:	14%
Distance > 5%:	2.3 miles	Distance > 10%:	0.1 mi
Steepest mile:	8.8%	Steepest 3 miles:	NA
Traffic:	2	Descent:	2

North Carolina

Pilot Mountain

Total elevation:	1,077ft	Length:	2.3 mi
Top elevation:	2,198 ft	Average grade:	8.8%
Minimum grade:	0%	Maximum grade:	16%
Distance > 5%:	2.0 miles	Distance > 10%:	0.6 mi
Steepest mile:	11.3%	Steepest 3 miles:	NA
Traffic:	2	Descent:	4

Sauratown Mountain

Total elevation:	946 ft	Length:	2.6 mi
Top elevation:	2,145 ft	Average grade:	6.9%
Minimum grade:	0%	Maximum grade:	19%
Distance > 5%:	2.2 miles	Distance > 10%:	0.2 mi
Steepest mile:	8.1%	Steepest 3 miles:	NA
Traffic:	1	Descent:	2

89/18

Total elevation:	1,131 ft	Length:	3.4 mi
Top elevation:	2,627 ft	Average grade:	6.3%
Minimum grade:	0%	Maximum grade:	8%
Distance > 5%:	2.8 miles	Distance > 10%:	0.0 mi
Steepest mile:	6.7%	Steepest 3 miles:	6.5 mi
Traffic:	2	Descent:	2

21 East

Total elevation:	1,420 ft	Length:	4.9 mi
Top elevation:	2,972 ft	Average grade:	5.5%
Minimum grade:	2%	Maximum grade:	8%
Distance > 5%:	3.9 miles	Distance > 10%:	0.0 mi
Steepest mile:	6.2%	Steepest 3 miles:	5.7%
Traffic:	2	Descent:	2

16 East

Total elevation:	1,807 ft		Length:	5.7 mi
Top elevation:	3,100 ft		Average grade:	6.0%
Minimum grade:	0%		Maximum grade:	9%
Distance > 5%:	4.2 miles		Distance > 10%:	0.0 mi
Steepest mile:	6.5%		Steepest 3 miles:	6.3%
Traffic:	2		Descent:	3

18 East

Total elevation:	1,590 ft		Length:	4.4 mi
Top elevation:	3,060 ft		Average grade:	6.7%
Minimum grade:	4%		Maximum grade:	8%
Distance > 5%:	3.9 miles		Distance > 10%:	0.0 mi
Steepest mile:	7.1%		Steepest 3 miles:	6.9%
Traffic:	2		Descent:	3

Mount Jefferson

Total elevation:	1,335 ft		Length:	3.2 mi
Top elevation:	4,476 ft		Average grade:	7.9%
Minimum grade:	4%		Maximum grade:	11%
Distance > 5%:	3.0 miles		Distance > 10%:	0.1 mi
Steepest mile:	8.5%		Steepest 3 miles:	8.0%
Traffic:	1		Descent:	4

Snake Mountain North

Total elevation:	1,054 ft	Length:	2.7 mi
Top elevation:	4,490 ft	Average grade:	7.4%
Minimum grade:	3%	Maximum grade:	10%
Distance > 5%:	2.2 miles	Distance > 10%:	0.0 mi
Steepest mile:	7.8%	Steepest 3 miles:	NA
Traffic:	2	Descent:	3

Snake Mountain South

Total elevation:	1,102 ft	Length:	2.9 mi
Top elevation:	4,490 ft	Average grade:	7.2%
Minimum grade:	0%	Maximum grade:	17%
Distance > 5%:	2.2 miles	Distance > 10%:	0.1 mi
Steepest mile:	8.7%	Steepest 3 miles:	NA
Traffic:	2	Descent:	3

Hawksnest

Total elevation:	1,521ft	Length:	3.8 mi
Top elevation:	4,732 ft	Average grade:	7.6%
Minimum grade:	0%	Maximum grade:	16%
Distance > 5%:	2.7 miles	Distance > 10%:	0.3 mi
Steepest mile:	9.2%	Steepest 3 miles:	7.8%
Traffic:	2	Descent:	4

Seven Devils

Total elevation:	1,089ft	Length:	1.9 mi
Top elevation:	4,300 ft	Average grade:	10.9%
Minimum grade:	1%	Maximum grade:	18%
Distance > 5%:	1.7 miles	Distance > 10%:	1.1 mi
Steepest mile:	11.3%	Steepest 3 miles:	NA
Traffic:	2	Descent:	5

Beech Mountain

Total elevation:	1,653 ft	Length:	3.5 mi
Top elevation:	5,285 ft	Average grade:	9.2%
Minimum grade:	1%	Maximum grade:	17%
Distance > 5%:	3.0 miles	Distance > 10%:	0.9 mi
Steepest mile:	9.5%	Steepest 3 miles:	9.3%
Traffic:	3	Descent:	4

Roan Mountain South

Total elevation:	2,927 ft	Length:	8.1 mi
Top elevation:	6,101 ft	Average grade:	6.8%
Minimum grade:	3%	Maximum grade:	9%
Distance > 5%:	6.9 miles	Distance > 10%:	0.0 mi
Steepest mile:	7.3%	Steepest 3 miles:	7.0%
Traffic:	2	Descent:	3

181 East

Total elevation:	2,663 ft	Length:	12.6 mi
Top elevation:	3,788 ft	Average grade:	4.0%
Minimum grade:	0%	Maximum grade:	9%
Distance > 5%:	5.7 miles	Distance > 10%:	0.0 mi
Steepest mile:	6.5%	Steepest 3 miles:	5.9%
Traffic:	2	Descent:	2

226 East

Total elevation:	1,377 ft	Length:	4.1 mi
Top elevation:	2,820 ft	Average grade:	6.4%
Minimum grade:	3%	Maximum grade:	8%
Distance > 5%:	2.9 miles	Distance > 10%:	0.0 mi
Steepest mile:	6.8%	Steepest 3 miles:	6.6%
Traffic:	2	Descent:	3

226A

Total elevation:	1,955 ft	Length:	9.7 mi
Top elevation:	3,398 ft	Average grade:	3.8%
Minimum grade:	0%	Maximum grade:	8%
Distance > 5%:	2.2 miles	Distance > 10%:	0.0 mi
Steepest mile:	5.7%	Steepest 3 miles:	5.4%
Traffic:	2	Descent:	4

Mount Mitchell

Total elevation:	5,161 ft	**Length:**	24.4 mi
Top elevation:	6,586 ft	**Average grade:**	4.0%
Minimum grade:	0%	**Maximum grade:**	9%
Distance > 5%:	10.7 miles	**Distance > 10%:**	0.0 mi
Steepest mile:	6.6%	**Steepest 3 miles:**	5.9%
Traffic:	2	**Descent:**	3

226 East (TN border)

Total elevation:	959 ft	**Length:**	4.3 mi
Top elevation:	3,730 ft	**Average grade:**	4.2%
Minimum grade:	1%	**Maximum grade:**	9%
Distance > 5%:	1.7 miles	**Distance > 10%:**	0.0 mi
Steepest mile:	5.6%	**Steepest 3 miles:**	4.3%
Traffic:	1	**Descent:**	3

Craggy Gardens

Total elevation:	2,978 ft	**Length:**	16.2 mi
Top elevation:	5,158 ft	**Average grade:**	3.5%
Minimum grade:	0%	**Maximum grade:**	9%
Distance > 5%:	5.5 miles	**Distance > 10%:**	0.0 mi
Steepest mile:	6.1%	**Steepest 3 miles:**	5.6%
Traffic:	1	**Descent:**	2

Town Mountain Road

Total elevation:	771 ft	Length:	1.8 mi
Top elevation:	3,068 ft	Average grade:	8.1%
Minimum grade:	4%	Maximum grade:	10%
Distance > 5%:	1.6 miles	Distance > 10%:	0.0 mi
Steepest mile:	8.2%	Steepest 3 miles:	NA
Traffic:	2	Descent:	3

Doggett Gap East

Total elevation:	1,412 ft	Length:	3.1 mi
Top elevation:	3,871 ft	Average grade:	8.6%
Minimum grade:	4%	Maximum grade:	10%
Distance > 5%:	2.9 miles	Distance > 10%:	0.2 mi
Steepest mile:	8.9%	Steepest 3 miles:	8.6%
Traffic:	1	Descent:	4

Doggett Gap West

Total elevation:	1,181 ft	Length:	3.4 mi
Top elevation:	3,871 ft	Average grade:	6.6%
Minimum grade:	3%	Maximum grade:	8%
Distance > 5%:	2.8 miles	Distance > 10%:	0.0 mi
Steepest mile:	7.1%	Steepest 3 miles:	6.7%
Traffic:	1	Descent:	3

Betsy Gap East

Total elevation:	1,188 ft	Length:	3.5 mi
Top elevation:	3,907 ft	Average grade:	6.4%
Minimum grade:	3%	Maximum grade:	9%
Distance > 5%:	2.7 miles	Distance > 10%:	0.0 mi
Steepest mile:	6.8%	Steepest 3 miles:	6.5%
Traffic:	1	Descent:	3

Betsy Gap West

Total elevation:	1,276 ft	Length:	3.9 mi
Top elevation:	3,907 ft	Average grade:	6.2%
Minimum grade:	3%	Maximum grade:	9%
Distance > 5%:	2.9 miles	Distance > 10%:	0.0 mi
Steepest mile:	6.8%	Steepest 3 miles:	6.5%
Traffic:	1	Descent:	3

Mount Pisgah

Total elevation:	2,914 ft	Length:	14.3 mi
Top elevation:	4,966 ft	Average grade:	3.9%
Minimum grade:	2%	Maximum grade:	8%
Distance > 5%:	3.0 miles	Distance > 10%:	0.0 mi
Steepest mile:	5.9%	Steepest 3 miles:	5.3%
Traffic:	2	Descent:	3

151/Mount Pisgah

Total elevation:	2,340 ft	Length:	6.1 mi
Top elevation:	4,966 ft	Average grade:	7.3%
Minimum grade:	3%	Maximum grade:	10%
Distance > 5%:	2.2 miles	Distance > 10%:	0.0 mi
Steepest mile:	8.4%	Steepest 3 miles:	8.2%
Traffic:	1	Descent:	4

276 South

Total elevation:	2,244 ft	Length:	9.9 mi
Top elevation:	4,542 ft	Average grade:	4.3%
Minimum grade:	2%	Maximum grade:	7%
Distance > 5%:	1.4 miles	Distance > 10%:	0.0 mi
Steepest mile:	5.3%	Steepest 3 miles:	4.8%
Traffic:	2	Descent:	3

276 North

Total elevation:	1,177 ft	Length:	3.8 mi
Top elevation:	4,542 ft	Average grade:	5.9%
Minimum grade:	4%	Maximum grade:	9%
Distance > 5%:	3.5 miles	Distance > 10%:	0.0 mi
Steepest mile:	6.8%	Steepest 3 miles:	6.1%
Traffic:	2	Descent:	3

215 South

Total elevation:	2,449 ft	Length:	7.8 mi
Top elevation:	5,343 ft	Average grade:	6.0%
Minimum grade:	3%	Maximum grade:	8%
Distance > 5%:	6.9 miles	Distance > 10%:	0.0 mi
Steepest mile:	6.5%	Steepest 3 miles:	6.1%
Traffic:	1	Descent:	2

215 North

Total elevation:	2,219 ft	Length:	8.7 mi
Top elevation:	4,343 ft	Average grade:	4.9%
Minimum grade:	4%	Maximum grade:	8%
Distance > 5%:	2.2 miles	Distance > 10%:	0.0 mi
Steepest mile:	5.6%	Steepest 3 miles:	5.2%
Traffic:	1	Descent:	3

Richland Balsam

Total elevation:	2,644 ft	Length:	11.7 mi
Top elevation:	6,040 ft	Average grade:	4.3%
Minimum grade:	1%	Maximum grade:	8%
Distance > 5%:	5.2 miles	Distance > 10%:	0.0 mi
Steepest mile:	6.5%	Steepest 3 miles:	5.6%
Traffic:	2	Descent:	3

Waterrock Knob East

Total elevation:	2,376 ft	Length:	8.7 mi
Top elevation:	5,772 ft	Average grade:	5.2%
Minimum grade:	3%	Maximum grade:	8%
Distance > 5%:	5.9 miles	Distance > 10%:	0.0 mi
Steepest mile:	5.8%	Steepest 3 miles:	5.4%
Traffic:	2	Descent:	1

19 South/Waterrock Knob

Total elevation:	3,580 ft	Length:	12.6 mi
Top elevation:	5,772 ft	Average grade:	5.4%
Minimum grade:	3%	Maximum grade:	8%
Distance > 5%:	10.6 miles	Distance > 10%:	0.0 mi
Steepest mile:	6.5%	Steepest 3 miles:	5.8%
Traffic:	2	Descent:	3

19 North/Waterrock Knob

Total elevation:	2,560 ft	Length:	8.0 mi
Top elevation:	5,772 ft	Average grade:	6.1%
Minimum grade:	3%	Maximum grade:	8%
Distance > 5%:	7.3 miles	Distance > 10%:	0.0 mi
Steepest mile:	7.2%	Steepest 3 miles:	7.1%
Traffic:	2	Descent:	3

Cherokee Hill

Total elevation:	3,155 ft		Length:	10.4 mi
Top elevation:	5,153 ft		Average grade:	5.7%
Minimum grade:	0%		Maximum grade:	8%
Distance > 5%:	5.6 miles		Distance > 10%:	0.0 mi
Steepest mile:	6.1%		Steepest 3 miles:	5.8%
Traffic:	1		Descent:	3

Clingmans Dome East

Total elevation:	4,269 ft		Length:	22.5 mi
Top elevation:	6,311 ft		Average grade:	3.6%
Minimum grade:	0%		Maximum grade:	8%
Distance > 5%:	5.8 miles		Distance > 10%:	0.0 mi
Steepest mile:	6.1%		Steepest 3 miles:	5.7%
Traffic:	3		Descent:	2

Cherohala Skyway East

Total elevation:	3,335 ft		Length:	11.6 mi
Top elevation:	5,300 ft		Average grade:	5.5%
Minimum grade:	0%		Maximum grade:	9%
Distance > 5%:	6.6 miles		Distance > 10%:	0.0 mi
Steepest mile:	6.5%		Steepest 3 miles:	6.1%
Traffic:	1		Descent:	2

Burkemont Road

Total elevation:	1,380 ft	Length:	2.7 mi
Top elevation:	2,540 ft	Average grade:	8.1%
Minimum grade:	4%	Maximum grade:	11%
Distance > 5%:	2.4 miles	Distance > 10%:	0.2 mi
Steepest mile:	9.4%	Steepest 3 miles:	NA
Traffic:	1	Descent:	3

Green River Cove Road

Total elevation:	970 ft	Length:	2.5 mi
Top elevation:	2,034 ft	Average grade:	7.5%
Minimum grade:	2%	Maximum grade:	12%
Distance > 5%:	2.0 miles	Distance > 10%:	0.1 mi
Steepest mile:	7.9%	Steepest 3 miles:	NA
Traffic:	1	Descent:	5

Howard Gap Road

Total elevation:	802 ft	Length:	1.4 mi
Top elevation:	1,905 ft	Average grade:	10.8%
Minimum grade:	4%	Maximum grade:	16%
Distance > 5%:	1.3 miles	Distance > 10%:	1.1 mi
Steepest mile:	13.9%	Steepest 3 miles:	NA
Traffic:	1	Descent:	2

Saluda Grade

Total elevation:	1,006 ft	Length:	3.6 mi
Top elevation:	2,140 ft	Average grade:	5.3%
Minimum grade:	2%	Maximum grade:	8%
Distance > 5%:	1.9 miles	Distance > 10%:	0.0 mi
Steepest mile:	6.1%	Steepest 3 miles:	5.5%
Traffic:	2	Descent:	3

South Carolina

Ceasars Head

Total elevation:	1,815 ft	Length:	5.6 mi
Top elevation:	3,199 ft	Average grade:	6.1%
Minimum grade:	3%	Maximum grade:	9%
Distance > 5%:	3.6 miles	Distance > 10%:	0.0 mi
Steepest mile:	7.0%	Steepest 3 miles:	6.4%
Traffic:	2	Descent:	4

Paris Mountain West

Total elevation:	813 ft		Length:	2.3 mi
Top elevation:	1,966 ft		Average grade:	6.7%
Minimum grade:	3%		Maximum grade:	10%
Distance > 5%:	1.9 miles		Distance > 10%:	0.0 mi
Steepest mile:	7.1%		Steepest 3 miles:	NA
Traffic:	1		Descent:	3

Tennessee

Stoney Fork Road East - lack of data

Roan Mountain North

Total elevation:	3,097 ft		Length:	9.0 mi
Top elevation:	6,101 ft		Average grade:	6.5%
Minimum grade:	3%		Maximum grade:	9%
Distance > 5%:	6.3 miles		Distance > 10%:	0.0 mi
Steepest mile:	7.2%		Steepest 3 miles:	6.7%
Traffic:	2		Descent:	3

107 West

Total elevation:	1,262 ft	Length:	4.1 mi
Top elevation:	3,730 ft	Average grade:	5.8%
Minimum grade:	1%	Maximum grade:	9%
Distance > 5%:	2.9 miles	Distance > 10%:	0.0 mi
Steepest mile:	6.2%	Steepest 3 miles:	6.0%
Traffic:	1	Descent:	3

19 West

Total elevation:	1,233 ft	Length:	5.2 mi
Top elevation:	3,290 ft	Average grade:	4.5%
Minimum grade:	4%	Maximum grade:	9%
Distance > 5%:	1.8 miles	Distance > 10%:	0.0 mi
Steepest mile:	6.1%	Steepest 3 miles:	5.5%
Traffic:	1	Descent:	3

Clingmans Dome West

Total elevation:	4,826 ft	Length:	20.1 mi
Top elevation:	6,311 ft	Average grade:	4.6%
Minimum grade:	0%	Maximum grade:	8%
Distance > 5%:	8.8 miles	Distance > 10%:	0.0 mi
Steepest mile:	6.3%	Steepest 3 miles:	5.8%
Traffic:	3	Descent:	3

Cherohala Skyway West – lack of data

Lookout Mountain (Rock City)

Total elevation:	957 ft	Length:	2.9 mi
Top elevation:	1,659 ft	Average grade:	6.3%
Minimum grade:	0%	Maximum grade:	10%
Distance > 5%:	2.0 miles	Distance > 10%:	0.1 mi
Steepest mile:	8.3%	Steepest 3 miles:	NA
Traffic:	3	Descent:	4

Ochs Highway

Total elevation:	1,437 ft	Length:	3.5 mi
Top elevation:	2,139 ft	Average grade:	7.8%
Minimum grade:	0%	Maximum grade:	10%
Distance > 5%:	2.9 miles	Distance > 10%:	0.1 mi
Steepest mile:	8.3%	Steepest 3 miles:	7.9%
Traffic:	2	Descent:	4

Ochs Highway/Sanders Rd/Scenic Highway

Total elevation:	2,127 ft	Length:	3.7 mi
Top elevation:	1,425 ft	Average grade:	7.3%
Minimum grade:	0%	Maximum grade:	10%
Distance > 5%:	3.0 miles	Distance > 10%:	0.1 mi
Steepest mile:	8.3%	Steepest 3 miles:	7.4%
Traffic:	2	Descent:	3

Scenic Highway

Total elevation:	1,248 ft	Length:	3.4 mi
Top elevation:	2,127 ft	Average grade:	7.0%
Minimum grade:	3%	Maximum grade:	9%
Distance > 5%:	2.9 miles	Distance > 10%:	0.0 mi
Steepest mile:	7.5%	Steepest 3 miles:	7.2%
Traffic:	3	Descent:	3

318/Scenic Highway

Total elevation:	1,449 ft	Length:	4.2 mi
Top elevation:	2,127 ft	Average grade:	6.5%
Minimum grade:	1%	Maximum grade:	10%
Distance > 5%:	3.1 miles	Distance > 10%:	0.0 mi
Steepest mile:	7.5%	Steepest 3 miles:	7.0%
Traffic:	2	Descent:	3

Elder Mountain Road

Total elevation:	1,147 ft	Length:	2.7 mi
Top elevation:	1,842 ft	Average grade:	8.0%
Minimum grade:	3%	Maximum grade:	10%
Distance > 5%:	2.3 miles	Distance > 10%:	0.0 mi
Steepest mile:	8.4%	Steepest 3 miles:	NA
Traffic:	2	Descent:	2

Raccoon Mountain

Total elevation:	1,063 ft	Length:	2.7 mi
Top elevation:	1,758 ft	Average grade:	7.5%
Minimum grade:	1%	Maximum grade:	9%
Distance > 5%:	2.1 miles	Distance > 10%:	0.0 mi
Steepest mile:	7.8%	Steepest 3 miles:	NA
Traffic:	2	Descent:	3

Signal Mountain

Total elevation:	1,249 ft	Length:	4.3 mi
Top elevation:	1,906 ft	Average grade:	5.5%
Minimum grade:	3%	Maximum grade:	8%
Distance > 5%:	2.9 miles	Distance > 10%:	0.0 mi
Steepest mile:	6.4%	Steepest 3 miles:	6.0%
Traffic:	3	Descent:	3

W Road

Total elevation:	1,213 ft	Length:	3.4 mi
Top elevation:	1,914 ft	Average grade:	6.8%
Minimum grade:	3%	Maximum grade:	11%
Distance > 5%:	2.5 miles	Distance > 10%:	0.0 mi
Steepest mile:	7.2%	Steepest 3 miles:	6.9%
Traffic:	2	Descent:	3

Suck Creek Road

Total elevation:	1,148 ft	Length:	4.1 mi
Top elevation:	1,842 ft	Average grade:	5.3%
Minimum grade:	3%	Maximum grade:	8%
Distance > 5%:	2.8 miles	Distance > 10%:	0.0 mi
Steepest mile:	6.3%	Steepest 3 miles:	5.5%
Traffic:	2	Descent:	2

27 West

Total elevation:	1,204 ft	Length:	4.2 mi
Top elevation:	1,928 ft	Average grade:	5.4%
Minimum grade:	3%	Maximum grade:	8%
Distance > 5%:	2.5 miles	Distance > 10%:	0.0 mi
Steepest mile:	6.2%	Steepest 3 miles:	5.6%
Traffic:	2	Descent:	2

127 West

Total elevation:	1,333 ft		Length:	4.3 mi
Top elevation:	2,053 ft		Average grade:	5.9%
Minimum grade:	3%		Maximum grade:	8%
Distance > 5%:	2.9 miles		Distance > 10%:	0.0 mi
Steepest mile:	6.6%		Steepest 3 miles:	6.2%
Traffic:	2		Descent:	2

Henson Gap Road

Total elevation:	933 ft		Length:	2.0 mi
Top elevation:	1,735 ft		Average grade:	8.8%
Minimum grade:	3%		Maximum grade:	14%
Distance > 5%:	1.8 miles		Distance > 10%:	0.1 mi
Steepest mile:	9.5%		Steepest 3 miles:	NA
Traffic:	1		Descent:	4

Robert Mills Road

Total elevation:	1,152 ft		Length:	2.1 mi
Top elevation:	1,878 ft		Average grade:	10.4%
Minimum grade:	4%		Maximum grade:	14%
Distance > 5%:	1.9 miles		Distance > 10%:	1.2mi
Steepest mile:	11.1%		Steepest 3 miles:	NA
Traffic:	2		Descent:	5

Montlake Road

Total elevation:	949 ft		Length:	2.3 mi
Top elevation:	1,705 ft		Average grade:	7.8%
Minimum grade:	3%		Maximum grade:	10%
Distance > 5%:	2.0 miles		Distance > 10%:	0.0 mi
Steepest mile:	8.5%		Steepest 3 miles:	NA%
Traffic:	2		Descent:	3

Mowbray Road

Total elevation:	924 ft		Length:	2.5 mi
Top elevation:	1,663 ft		Average grade:	7.0%
Minimum grade:	3%		Maximum grade:	10%
Distance > 5%:	1.7 miles		Distance > 10%:	0.0 mi
Steepest mile:	7.6%		Steepest 3 miles:	NA
Traffic:	2		Descent:	3

Brayton Mountain Road

Total elevation:	876 ft		Length:	2.2 mi
Top elevation:	1,742 ft		Average grade:	7.5%
Minimum grade:	3%		Maximum grade:	11%
Distance > 5%:	1.9 miles		Distance > 10%:	0.1 mi
Steepest mile:	7.8%		Steepest 3 miles:	NA
Traffic:	1		Descent:	4

Fredonia Road

Total elevation:	1,127 ft	Length:	2.9 mi
Top elevation:	1,887 ft	Average grade:	7.4%
Minimum grade:	3%	Maximum grade:	11%
Distance > 5%:	2.4 miles	Distance > 10%:	0.1 mi
Steepest mile:	7.8%	Steepest 3 miles:	NA
Traffic:	2	Descent:	3

Daus Mountain Road

Total elevation:	1,220 ft	Length:	2.8 mi
Top elevation:	1,923 ft	Average grade:	8.3%
Minimum grade:	3%	Maximum grade:	17%
Distance > 5%:	2.2 miles	Distance > 10%:	0.5 mi
Steepest mile:	10.3%	Steepest 3 miles:	NA
Traffic:	1	Descent:	4

108 East

Total elevation:	1,032 ft	Length:	3.2 mi
Top elevation:	1,726 ft	Average grade:	6.1%
Minimum grade:	2%	Maximum grade:	9%
Distance > 5%:	2.7 miles	Distance > 10%:	0.0 mi
Steepest mile:	6.6%	Steepest 3 miles:	6.2%
Traffic:	2	Descent:	2

Sequatchie Mountain Road

Total elevation:	1,049 ft	**Length:**	1.8 mi
Top elevation:	1,719 ft	**Average grade:**	11.0%
Minimum grade:	5%	**Maximum grade:**	13%
Distance > 5%:	1.6 miles	**Distance > 10%:**	1.3 mi
Steepest mile:	11.3%	**Steepest 3 miles:**	NA
Traffic:	1	**Descent:**	4

156 East

Total elevation:	1,039 ft	**Length:**	2.1 mi
Top elevation:	1,741 ft	**Average grade:**	9.4%
Minimum grade:	4%	**Maximum grade:**	12%
Distance > 5%:	1.9 miles	**Distance > 10%:**	0.2 mi
Steepest mile:	9.7%	**Steepest 3 miles:**	NA
Traffic:	2	**Descent:**	4

Virginia

33 East

Total elevation:	1,416 ft	Length:	4.1 mi
Top elevation:	3,458 ft	Average grade:	6.5%
Minimum grade:	4%	Maximum grade:	9%
Distance > 5%:	3.2 miles	Distance > 10%:	0.0 mi
Steepest mile:	6.8%	Steepest 3 miles:	6.6%
Traffic:	2	Descent:	3

Reddish Knob

Total elevation:	2,635 ft	Length:	9.1 mi
Top elevation:	4,369 ft	Average grade:	5.5%
Minimum grade:	0%	Maximum grade:	10%
Distance > 5%:	6.5 miles	Distance > 10%:	0.0 mi
Steepest mile:	7.4%	Steepest 3 miles:	7.1%
Traffic:	1	Descent:	3

250 East

Total elevation:	1,267 ft	Length:	4.4 mi
Top elevation:	4,352 ft	Average grade:	5.5%
Minimum grade:	0%	Maximum grade:	8%
Distance > 5%:	2.4 miles	Distance > 10%:	0.0 mi
Steepest mile:	6.4%	Steepest 3 miles:	6.0%
Traffic:	2	Descent:	3

606 East

Total elevation:	1,777 ft	Length:	4.2 mi
Top elevation:	3,331 ft	Average grade:	8.0%
Minimum grade:	2%	Maximum grade:	12%
Distance > 5%:	3.6 miles	Distance > 10%:	0.6 mi
Steepest mile:	9.2%	Steepest 3 miles:	8.5%
Traffic:	1	Descent:	4

Wintergreen

Total elevation:	2,664 ft	Length:	6.1 mi
Top elevation:	3,833 ft	Average grade:	8.3%
Minimum grade:	2%	Maximum grade:	13%
Distance > 5%:	4.7 miles	Distance > 10%:	0.8 mi
Steepest mile:	10.7%	Steepest 3 miles:	8.6%
Traffic:	2	Descent:	4

Reeds Gap East

Total elevation:	1,468 ft	Length:	3.1 mi
Top elevation:	2,637 ft	Average grade:	9.0%
Minimum grade:	3%	Maximum grade:	14%
Distance > 5%:	2.1 miles	Distance > 10%:	1.1 mi
Steepest mile:	11.3%	Steepest 3 miles:	9.1%
Traffic:	2	Descent:	1

Reeds Gap West

Total elevation:	924 ft	Length:	2.0 mi
Top elevation:	2,637 ft	Average grade:	8.7%
Minimum grade:	3%	Maximum grade:	11%
Distance > 5%:	1.7 miles	Distance > 10%:	0.1 mi
Steepest mile:	9.2%	Steepest 3 miles:	NA
Traffic:	1	Descent:	3

Vesuvius

Total elevation:	1,683 ft	Length:	4.2 mi
Top elevation:	3,111 ft	Average grade:	7.6%
Minimum grade:	0%	Maximum grade:	14%
Distance > 5%:	3.4 miles	Distance > 10%:	0.7 mi
Steepest mile:	11.1%	Steepest 3 miles:	9.2%
Traffic:	1	Descent:	4

56 East

Total elevation:	1,964 ft	Length:	8.1 mi
Top elevation:	3,111 ft	Average grade:	4.6%
Minimum grade:	0%	Maximum grade:	10%
Distance > 5%:	4.8 miles	Distance > 10%:	0.0 mi
Steepest mile:	6.8%	Steepest 3 miles:	5.9%
Traffic:	1	Descent:	3

Thunder Hill

Total elevation:	3,246 ft	Length:	12.2 mi
Top elevation:	3,908 ft	Average grade:	5.0%
Minimum grade:	2%	Maximum grade:	8%
Distance > 5%:	2.2 miles	Distance > 10%:	0.0 mi
Steepest mile:	6.4%	Steepest 3 miles:	5.8%
Traffic:	1	Descent:	2

43 South

Total elevation:	1,336 ft	Length:	3.0 mi
Top elevation:	2,574 ft	Average grade:	8.4%
Minimum grade:	4%	Maximum grade:	10%
Distance > 5%:	2.6 miles	Distance > 10%:	0.0 mi
Steepest mile:	8.6%	Steepest 3 miles:	8.4%
Traffic:	1	Descent:	3

695 South

Total elevation:	1,116 ft	Length:	2.3 mi
Top elevation:	2,251 ft	Average grade:	9.2%
Minimum grade:	4%	Maximum grade:	14%
Distance > 5%:	2.1 miles	Distance > 10%:	0.2 mi
Steepest mile:	9.4%	Steepest 3 miles:	NA
Traffic:	1	Descent:	4

43 North

Total elevation:	1,409 ft	Length:	4.1 mi
Top elevation:	2,251 ft	Average grade:	6.5%
Minimum grade:	3%	Maximum grade:	8%
Distance > 5%:	2.6 miles	Distance > 10%:	0.0 mi
Steepest mile:	6.9%	Steepest 3 miles:	6.7%
Traffic:	1	Descent:	3

Mill Mountain

Total elevation:	775 ft	Length:	1.9 mi
Top elevation:	1,708 ft	Average grade:	7.7%
Minimum grade:	1%	Maximum grade:	11%
Distance > 5%:	1.5 miles	Distance > 10%:	0.1 mi
Steepest mile:	8.5%	Steepest 3 miles:	NA
Traffic:	1	Descent:	4

311 South (WV border)

Total elevation:	1,134 ft	Length:	3.4 mi
Top elevation:	3,004 ft	Average grade:	6.3%
Minimum grade:	3%	Maximum grade:	9%
Distance > 5%:	2.7 miles	Distance > 10%:	0.0 mi
Steepest mile:	6.8%	Steepest 3 miles:	6.4%
Traffic:	1	Descent:	3

311 North

Total elevation:	1,619 ft	Length:	5.5 mi
Top elevation:	3,470 ft	Average grade:	5.6%
Minimum grade:	4%	Maximum grade:	8%
Distance > 5%:	3.0 miles	Distance > 10%:	0.0 mi
Steepest mile:	6.4%	Steepest 3 miles:	5.9%
Traffic:	1	Descent:	3

311 South

Total elevation:	1,750 ft	Length:	4.8 mi
Top elevation:	3,470 ft	Average grade:	6.9%
Minimum grade:	4%	Maximum grade:	9%
Distance > 5%:	4.0 miles	Distance > 10%:	0.0 mi
Steepest mile:	7.4%	Steepest 3 miles:	7.0%
Traffic:	1	Descent:	3

Mountain Lake

Total elevation:	2,115 ft	Length:	6.4 mi
Top elevation:	3,931 ft	Average grade:	6.3%
Minimum grade:	3%	Maximum grade:	9%
Distance > 5%:	5.4 miles	Distance > 10%:	0.0 mi
Steepest mile:	7.3%	Steepest 3 miles:	6.7%
Traffic:	1	Descent:	3

613 (Doe Creek Road)

Total elevation:	1,895 ft	Length:	4.2 mi
Top elevation:	3,931 ft	Average grade:	8.6%
Minimum grade:	3%	Maximum grade:	13%
Distance > 5%:	3.7 miles	Distance > 10%:	0.5 mi
Steepest mile:	10.1%	Steepest 3 miles:	8.9%
Traffic:	1	Descent:	4

Little Walker Mountain South

Total elevation:	658 ft	Length:	1.7 mi
Top elevation:	2,738 ft	Average grade:	7.3%
Minimum grade:	3%	Maximum grade:	10%
Distance > 5%:	1.5 miles	Distance > 10%:	0.0 mi
Steepest mile:	7.6%	Steepest 3 miles:	NA
Traffic:	1	Descent:	3

Little Walker Mountain North

Total elevation:	692 ft	Length:	2.2 mi
Top elevation:	2,738 ft	Average grade:	6.0%
Minimum grade:	3%	Maximum grade:	8%
Distance > 5%:	1.6 miles	Distance > 10%:	0.0 mi
Steepest mile:	6.6%	Steepest 3 miles:	NA
Traffic:	1	Descent:	3

Walker Mountain South

Total elevation:	1,129 ft	Length:	3.3 mi
Top elevation:	3,175 ft	Average grade:	6.5%
Minimum grade:	3%	Maximum grade:	10%
Distance > 5%:	2.8 miles	Distance > 10%:	0.1 mi
Steepest mile:	7.2%	Steepest 3 miles:	6.7%
Traffic:	1	Descent:	5

Walker Mountain North

Total elevation:	703 ft	Length:	3.3 mi
Top elevation:	3,175 ft	Average grade:	4.0%
Minimum grade:	2%	Maximum grade:	8%
Distance > 5%:	1.5 miles	Distance > 10%:	0.0 mi
Steepest mile:	5.6%	Steepest 3 miles:	4.2%
Traffic:	1	Descent:	3

Squirrel Spur Road

Total elevation:	1,151 ft	Length:	2.9 mi
Top elevation:	2,664 ft	Average grade:	7.5%
Minimum grade:	3%	Maximum grade:	9%
Distance > 5%:	2.6 miles	Distance > 10%:	0.0 mi
Steepest mile:	7.8%	Steepest 3 miles:	NA
Traffic:	1	Descent:	3

Willis Gap

Total elevation:	1,223 ft	Length:	2.6 mi
Top elevation:	2,676 ft	Average grade:	8.9%
Minimum grade:	4%	Maximum grade:	11%
Distance > 5%:	2.3 miles	Distance > 10%:	0.1 mi
Steepest mile:	9.3%	Steepest 3 miles:	NA
Traffic:	1	Descent:	3

Orchard Gap

Total elevation:	983 ft	Length:	2.2 mi
Top elevation:	2,672 ft	Average grade:	8.5%
Minimum grade:	4%	Maximum grade:	15%
Distance > 5%:	2.0 miles	Distance > 10%:	0.2 mi
Steepest mile:	9.1%	Steepest 3 miles:	NA
Traffic:	1	Descent:	4

52 South (NC border)

Total elevation:	1,391 ft	Length:	4.5 mi
Top elevation:	2,935 ft	Average grade:	5.9%
Minimum grade:	3%	Maximum grade:	9%
Distance > 5%:	3.3 miles	Distance > 10%:	0.0 mi
Steepest mile:	6.8%	Steepest 3 miles:	6.3%
Traffic:	3	Descent:	2

Pipers Gap

Total elevation:	1,165 ft	Length:	2.9 mi
Top elevation:	2,738 ft	Average grade:	7.6%
Minimum grade:	3%	Maximum grade:	16%
Distance > 5%:	2.2 miles	Distance > 10%:	0.3 mi
Steepest mile:	9.3%	Steepest 3 miles:	NA
Traffic:	1	Descent:	4

58/Grayson Highlands

Total elevation:	1,743 ft	Length:	7.2 mi
Top elevation:	4,957 ft	Average grade:	4.6%
Minimum grade:	0%	Maximum grade:	9%
Distance > 5%:	2.5 miles	Distance > 10%:	0.0 mi
Steepest mile:	6.5%	Steepest 3 miles:	5.5%
Traffic:	2	Descent:	3

Whitetop Road South

Total elevation:	695 ft	Length:	1.7 mi
Top elevation:	4,562 ft	Average grade:	7.7%
Minimum grade:	4%	Maximum grade:	9%
Distance > 5%:	1.6 miles	Distance > 10%:	0.0 mi
Steepest mile:	8.1%	Steepest 3 miles:	NA
Traffic:	1	Descent:	3

Whitetop Road North

Total elevation:	1,311 ft	Length:	4.7 mi
Top elevation:	4,358 ft	Average grade:	5.3%
Minimum grade:	3%	Maximum grade:	7%
Distance > 5%:	2.4 miles	Distance > 10%:	0.0 mi
Steepest mile:	5.8%	Steepest 3 miles:	5.5%
Traffic:	1	Descent:	3

52 South

Total elevation:	1,140 ft	Length:	4.0 mi
Top elevation:	3,485 ft	Average grade:	5.4%
Minimum grade:	3%	Maximum grade:	8%
Distance > 5%:	2.4 miles	Distance > 10%:	0.0 mi
Steepest mile:	5.9%	Steepest 3 miles:	5.6%
Traffic:	1	Descent:	3

52 North

Total elevation:	843 ft	Length:	3.5 mi
Top elevation:	3,485 ft	Average grade:	4.6%
Minimum grade:	3%	Maximum grade:	8%
Distance > 5%:	1.5 miles	Distance > 10%:	0.0 mi
Steepest mile:	5.5%	Steepest 3 miles:	4.8%
Traffic:	1	Descent:	3

Big Mountain Road

Total elevation:	620 ft	Length:	2.4 mi
Top elevation:	3,493 ft	Average grade:	4.9%
Minimum grade:	3%	Maximum grade:	7%
Distance > 5%:	1.1 miles	Distance > 10%:	0.0 mi
Steepest mile:	5.6%	Steepest 3 miles:	NA
Traffic:	1	Descent:	2

16 South

Total elevation:	1,231 ft	Length:	3.5 mi
Top elevation:	3,446 ft	Average grade:	6.7%
Minimum grade:	3%	Maximum grade:	9%
Distance > 5%:	2.8 miles	Distance > 10%:	0.0 mi
Steepest mile:	7.1%	Steepest 3 miles:	6.8%
Traffic:	2	Descent:	3

16 North

Total elevation:	1,255 ft	Length:	3.3 mi
Top elevation:	3,446 ft	Average grade:	7.2%
Minimum grade:	3%	Maximum grade:	9%
Distance > 5%:	2.7 miles	Distance > 10%:	0.0 mi
Steepest mile:	7.5%	Steepest 3 miles:	7.3%
Traffic:	2	Descent:	3

High Knob

Total elevation:	1,577 ft	Length:	3.0 mi
Top elevation:	3,781 ft	Average grade:	10.0%
Minimum grade:	4%	Maximum grade:	14%
Distance > 5%:	2.7 miles	Distance > 10%:	1.4 mi
Steepest mile:	10.8%	Steepest 3 miles:	10.0%
Traffic:	1	Descent:	5

160 East

Total elevation:	1,657 ft	Length:	4.4 mi
Top elevation:	3,709 ft	Average grade:	7.1%
Minimum grade:	4%	Maximum grade:	9%
Distance > 5%:	4.0 miles	Distance > 10%:	0.0 mi
Steepest mile:	7.4%	Steepest 3 miles:	7.2%
Traffic:	2	Descent:	3

West Virginia

33 West (VA border)

Total elevation:	1,768 ft	Length:	5.5 mi
Top elevation:	3,458 ft	Average grade:	6.1%
Minimum grade:	3%	Maximum grade:	9%
Distance > 5%:	4.1 miles	Distance > 10%:	0.0 mi
Steepest mile:	7.2%	Steepest 3 miles:	6.8%
Traffic:	2	Descent:	3

33 West – lack of data

15 East – lack of data

Snowshoe East

Total elevation:	1,503 ft	Length:	4.4 mi
Top elevation:	4,806 ft	Average grade:	6.5%
Minimum grade:	0%	Maximum grade:	13%
Distance > 5%:	3.2 miles	Distance > 10%:	0.8 mi
Steepest mile:	11.1%	Steepest 3 miles:	6.3%
Traffic:	1	Descent:	3

Snowshoe West

Total elevation:	1,554 ft	Length:	4.9 mi
Top elevation:	4,683 ft	Average grade:	6.0%
Minimum grade:	3%	Maximum grade:	9%
Distance > 5%:	3.8 miles	Distance > 10%:	0.0 mi
Steepest mile:	6.8%	Steepest 3 miles:	6.3%
Traffic:	2	Descent:	3

219/150

Total elevation:	2,184 ft	Length:	9.2 mi
Top elevation:	4,299 ft	Average grade:	4.5%
Minimum grade:	1%	Maximum grade:	8%
Distance > 5%:	6.6 miles	Distance > 10%:	0.0 mi
Steepest mile:	6.4%	Steepest 3 miles:	5.9%
Traffic:	2	Descent:	3

39/150

Total elevation:	1,676 ft	Length:	5.7 mi
Top elevation:	4,251 ft	Average grade:	5.6%
Minimum grade:	2%	Maximum grade:	8%
Distance > 5%:	3.7 miles	Distance > 10%:	0.0 mi
Steepest mile:	6.4%	Steepest 3 miles:	6.0%
Traffic:	2	Descent:	2

Kenneson Mountain

Total elevation:	1,413 ft	Length:	5.2 mi
Top elevation:	3,988 ft	Average grade:	5.2%
Minimum grade:	2%	Maximum grade:	8%
Distance > 5%:	2.8 miles	Distance > 10%:	0.0 mi
Steepest mile:	6.4%	Steepest 3 miles:	5.6%
Traffic:	2	Descent:	2

311 North

Total elevation:	973 ft	Length:	3.1 mi
Top elevation:	3,004 ft	Average grade:	5.9%
Minimum grade:	3%	Maximum grade:	8%
Distance > 5%:	2.1 miles	Distance > 10%:	0.0 mi
Steepest mile:	6.4%	Steepest 3 miles:	5.9%
Traffic:	1	Descent:	3

Hill Climb Profiles (Top 50)
(in alphabetical order)

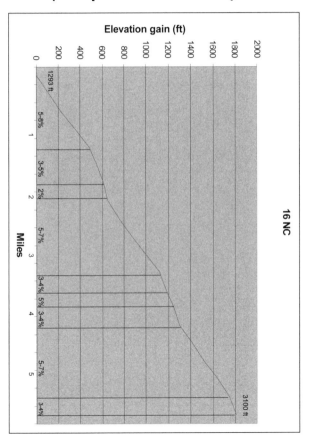

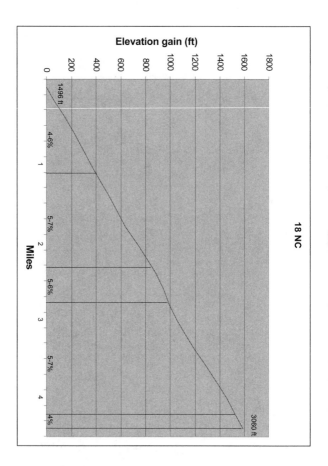

18 NC

Elevation gain (ft)

1496 ft

4-6%

5-7%

5-6%

5-7%

4%

3060 ft

Miles

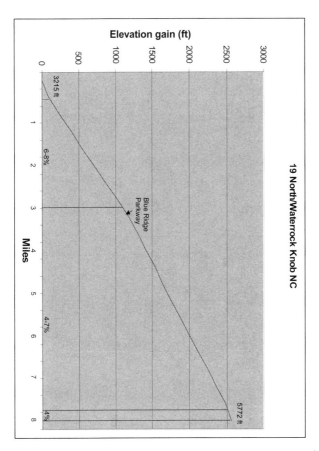

19 North/Waterrock Knob NC

Elevation gain (ft)

Miles

3215 ft

6-8%

Blue Ridge
Parkway

4-7%

4%

5772 ft

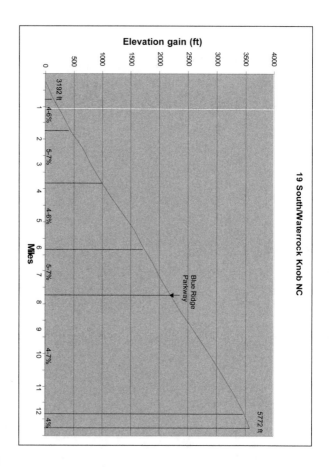

19 South/Waterrock Knob NC

Elevation gain (ft)

Miles

3192 ft

4.6%

5.7%

4.6%

5.7%

Blue Ridge
Parkway

4.7%

5772 ft

4%

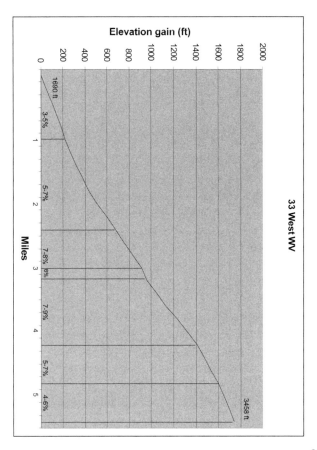

33 West WV

Elevation gain (ft)

Miles

1690 ft

3-5%

5-7%

7-8%

6%

7-9%

5-7%

4-6%

3458 ft

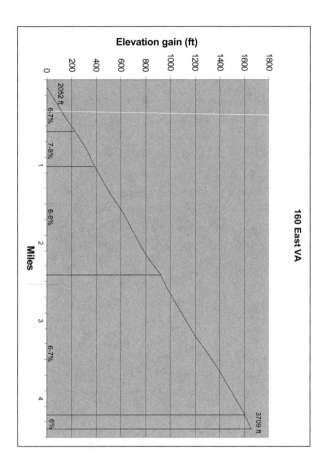

160 East VA

Elevation gain (ft)

Miles

2052 ft
6-7%
7-8%
6-8%
6-7%
6%
3709 ft

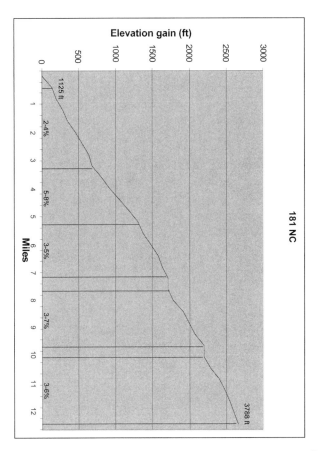

181 NC

Miles

1125 ft
2-4%
5-8%
3-5%
3-7%
3-6%
3788 ft

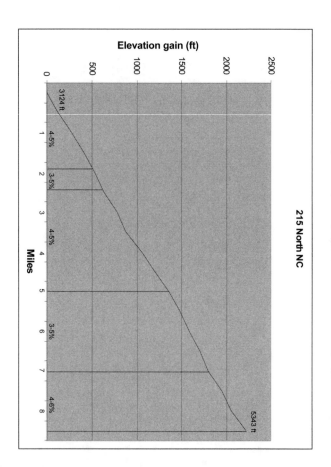

215 North NC

Elevation gain (ft)

3124 ft

4-5%

3-5%

4-5%

3-5%

4-6%

5343 ft

Miles

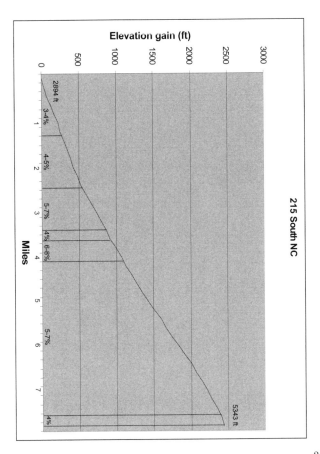

215 South NC

Elevation gain (ft)

2894 ft
3-4%
4-5%
5-7%
4% 6-8%
5-7%
5343 ft
4%

Miles

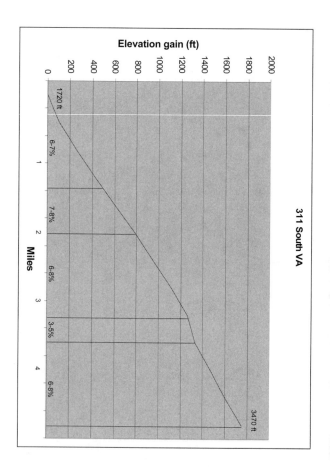

311 South VA

Elevation gain (ft)

Miles

1720 ft

6-7%

7-8%

6-8%

3-5%

6-8%

3470 ft

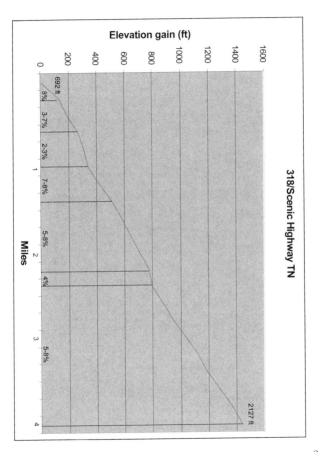

318/Scenic Highway TN

Elevation gain (ft)

Miles

692 ft
8%
3-7%
2-3%
7-8%
5-8%
4%
5-8%
2127 ft

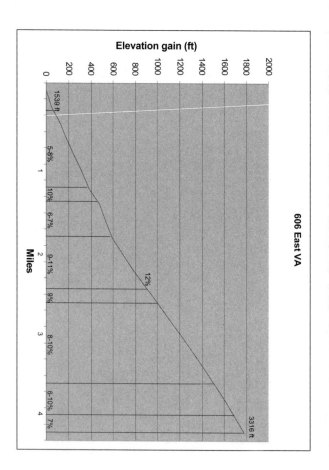

606 East VA

Elevation gain (ft)

1539 ft

5-8%

10%

6-7%

9-11%

12%

9%

8-10%

6-10%

7%

3316 ft

Miles

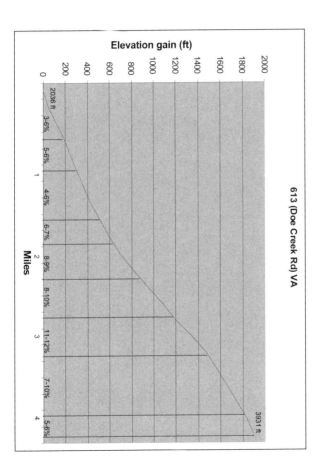

613 (Doe Creek Rd) VA

Elevation gain (ft)

Miles

2036 ft
3-6%
5-6%
4-6%
6-7%
8-9%
8-10%
11-12%
7-10%
5-6%
3931 ft

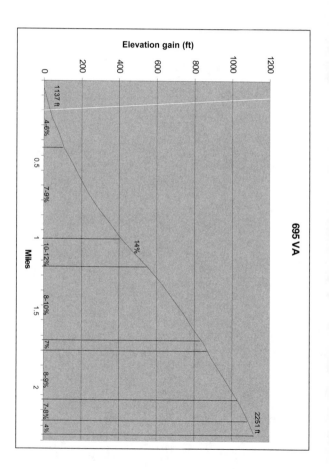

695 VA

Elevation gain (ft)

1137 ft

4-6%

7-9%

14%

10-12%

8-10%

7%

8-9%

7-8%

4%

2251 ft

Miles

214

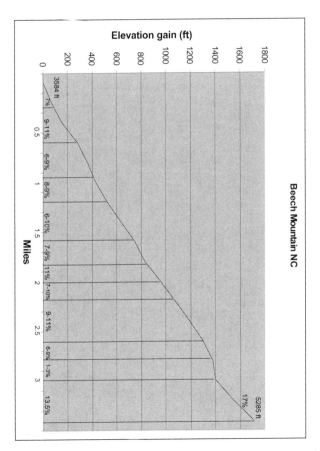

Beech Mountain NC

Elevation gain (ft)

Miles

3584 ft
7%
9-11%
6-9%
8-9%
6-10%
7-9%
11%
7-10%
9-11%
6-9%
1-3%
13.5%
17%
5285 ft

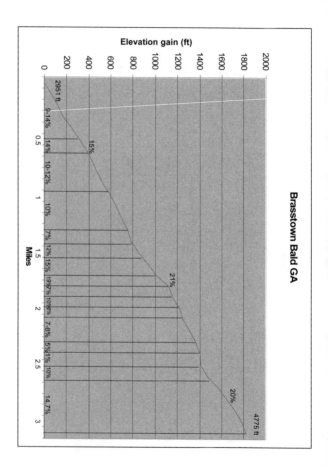

Brasstown Bald GA

Elevation gain (ft)

Miles

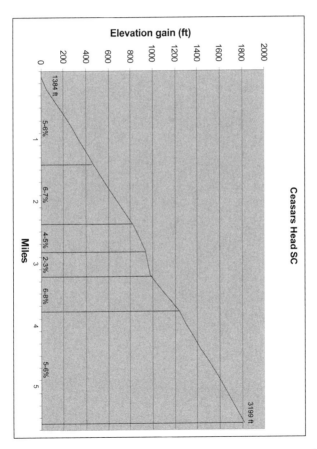

Ceasars Head SC

Elevation gain (ft)

Miles

1384 ft

5-6%

6-7%

4-5%

2-3%

6-8%

5-6%

3199 ft

217

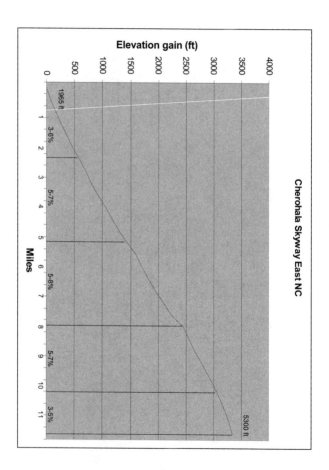

Cherohala Skyway East NC

Elevation gain (ft)

4000
3500
3000
2500
2000
1500
1000
500
0

1965 ft

3-6%

5-7%

5-8%

5-7%

3-5%

5300 ft

Miles

0 1 2 3 4 5 6 7 8 9 10 11

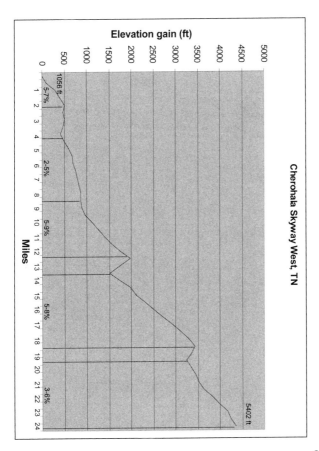

Cherohala Skyway West, TN

Elevation gain (ft)

1056 ft
5-7%
2-5%
5-9%
5-8%
3-6%
5402 ft

Miles

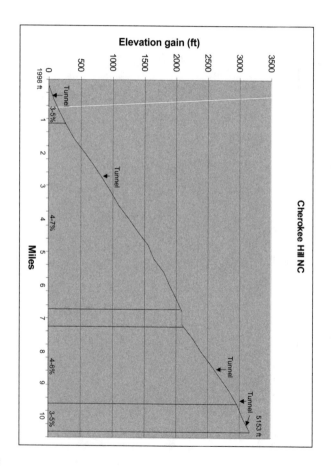

Cherokee Hill NC

Elevation gain (ft)

Miles

1998 ft

Tunnel

3-5%

Tunnel

4-7%

Tunnel

4-6%

Tunnel

3-5%

5153 ft

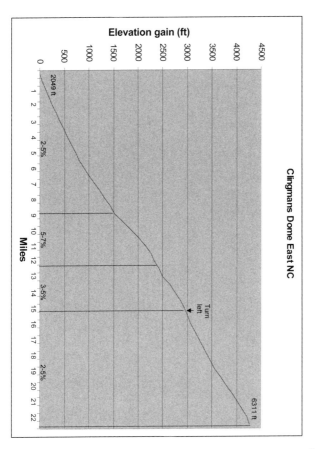

Clingmans Dome East NC

Elevation gain (ft)

2049 ft

2-5%

5-7%

3-5%

Turn left

2-5%

6311 ft

Miles

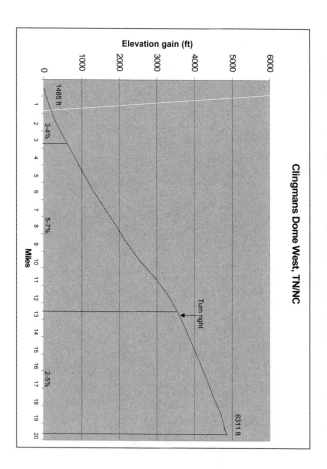

Clingmans Dome West, TN/NC

Elevation gain (ft)

1485 ft

3-4%

5-7%

Turn right

2-5%

6311 ft

Miles

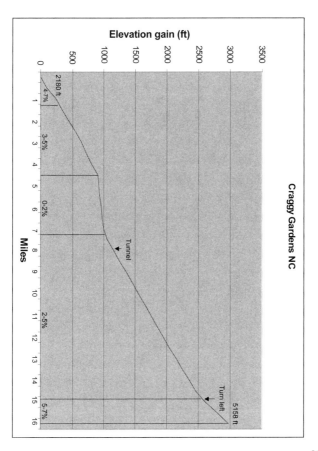

Craggy Gardens NC

Elevation gain (ft)

2180 ft
4.7%
3.5%
0.2%
Tunnel
2.5%
Turn left
5158 ft
5.7%

Miles

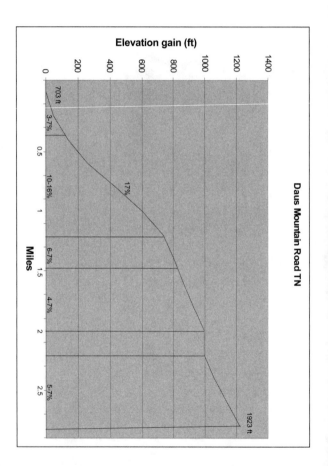

Daus Mountain Road TN

Elevation gain (ft)

703 ft
3-7%
10-16%
17%
6-7%
4-7%
5-7%
1923 ft

Miles

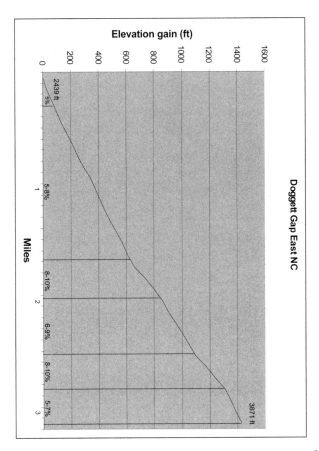

Doggett Gap East NC

Elevation gain (ft)

Miles

2439 ft
5%
5-8%
8-10%
6-9%
8-10%
5-7%
3871 ft

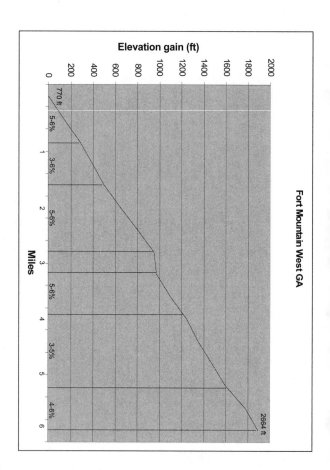

Fort Mountain West GA

Elevation gain (ft)

Miles

770 ft

5-6%

3-6%

5-6%

5-6%

3-5%

4-6%

2664 ft

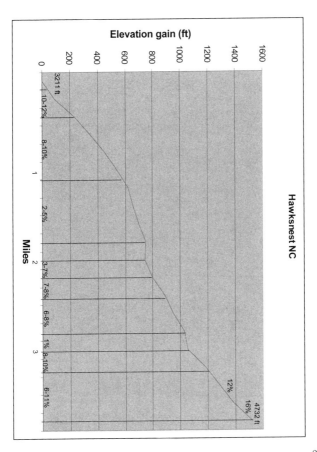

Hawksnest NC

Elevation gain (ft)

Miles

3211 ft
10-12%
8-10%
2-5%
3-7%
7-8%
6-8%
1%
8-10%
6-11%
12%
16%
4732 ft

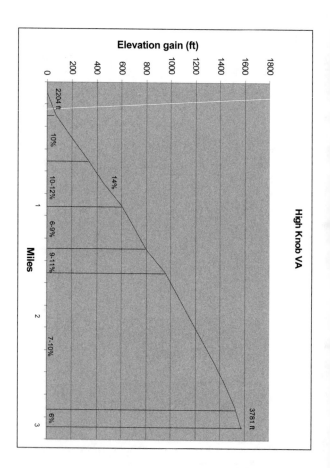

High Knob VA

Elevation gain (ft)

Miles

2204 ft

10%

10-12%

14%

6-9%

9-11%

7-10%

6%

3781 ft

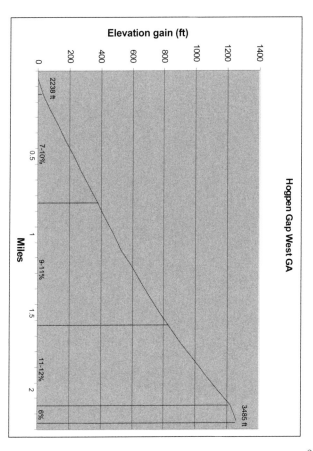

Hogpen Gap West GA

Elevation gain (ft)

Miles

2238 ft
7-10%
9-11%
11-12%
6%
3485 ft

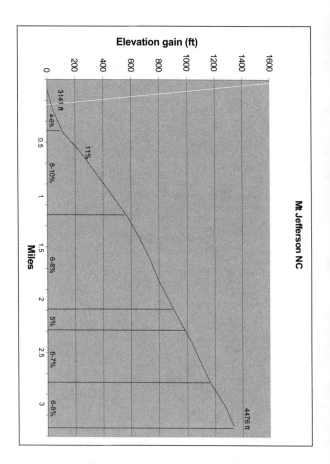

Mt Jefferson NC

Elevation gain (ft)

3141 ft

4476 ft

4-6%
11%
8-10%
6-8%
5%
6-7%
6-8%

Miles

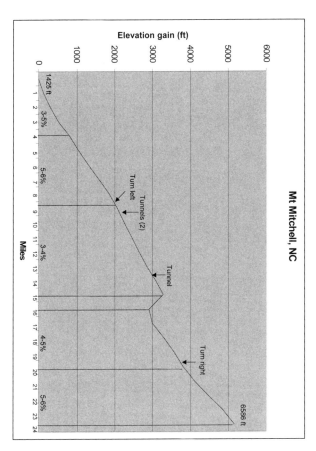

Mt Mitchell, NC

Elevation gain (ft)

1425 ft
3-5%
5-6%
Turn left
Tunnels (2)
3-4%
Tunnel
4-5%
Turn right
5-6%
6586 ft

Miles

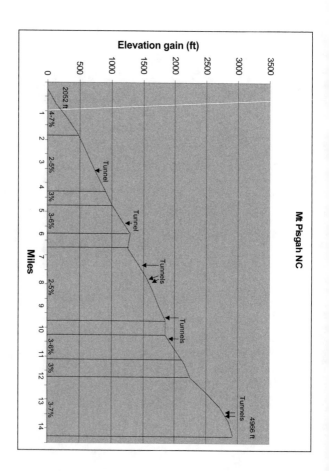

Mt Pisgah NC

Elevation gain (ft)

2052 ft

Tunnel

Tunnel

Tunnel

Tunnels

Tunnels

Tunnels

Tunnels

4966 ft

Miles

4-7% 2-5% 3% 3-6% 2-5% 3-6% 3% 3-7%

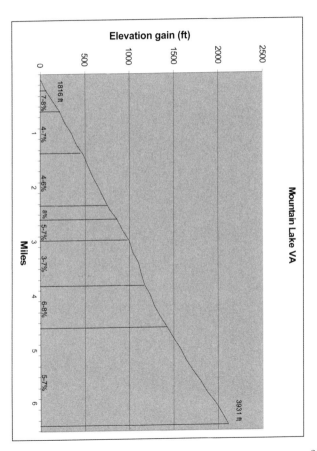

Mountain Lake VA

Elevation gain (ft)

Miles

1816 ft
7-8%
4-7%
4-6%
8%
5-7%
3-7%
6-8%
5-7%
3931 ft

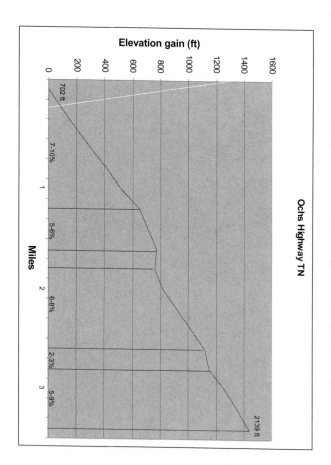

Ochs Highway TN

Elevation gain (ft)

Miles

702 ft

7-10%

5-6%

6-8%

2-3%

5-9%

2139 ft

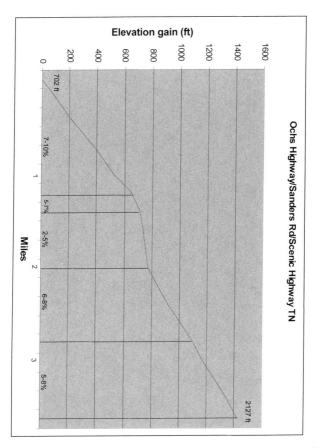

Ochs Highway/Sanders Rd/Scenic Highway TN

Elevation gain (ft)

Miles

702 ft

7-10%

5-7%

2-5%

6-8%

5-8%

2127 ft

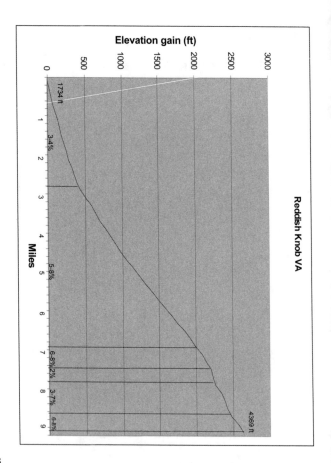

Reddish Knob VA

Elevation gain (ft)

Miles

1734 ft

3-4%

5-8%

6-8%/2%

3-7%

6-8%

4369 ft

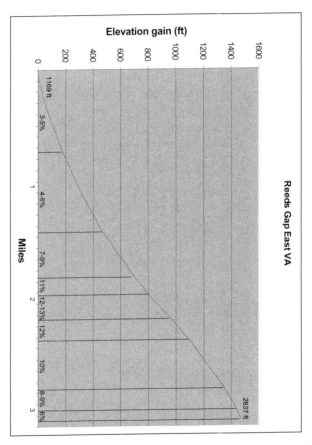

Reeds Gap East VA

Elevation gain (ft)

Miles

1169 ft
3-5%
4-6%
7-9%
11%
12-13%
12%
10%
8-9%
6%
2637 ft

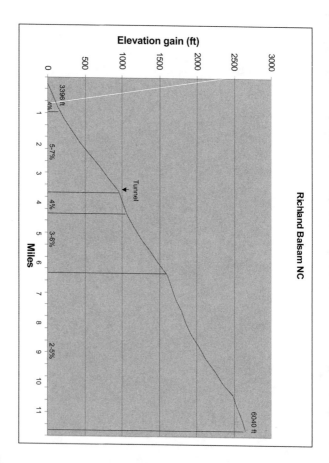

Richland Balsam NC

Elevation gain (ft)

Miles

3396 ft

4%

5-7%

Tunnel

4%

3-6%

2-5%

6040 ft

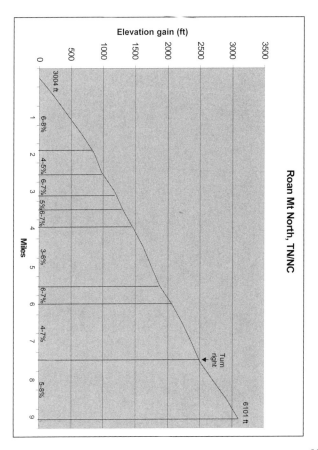

Roan Mt North, TN/NC

Elevation gain (ft)

3004 ft

6-8%
4-5%
6-7%
5%
6-7%
3-6%
6-7%
4-7%
Turn right
5-8%
6101 ft

Miles

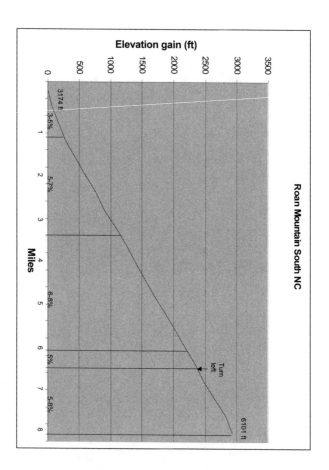

Roan Mountain South NC

Elevation gain (ft)

Miles

3174 ft
3-5%
5-7%
6-8%
5%
Turn left
5-8%
6101 ft

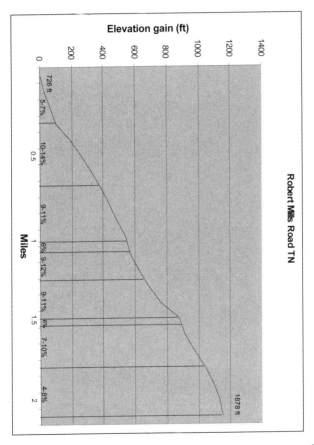

Robert Mills Road TN

Elevation gain (ft)

Miles

726 ft
5-7%
10-14%
9-11%
6%
9-12%
9-11%
6%
7-10%
4-8%
1878 ft

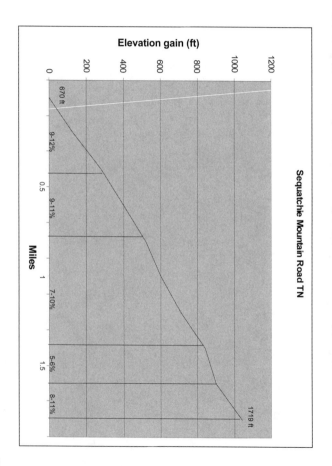

Sequatchie Mountain Road TN

Elevation gain (ft)

670 ft

9-12%

9-11%

7-10%

5-6%

8-11%

1719 ft

Miles

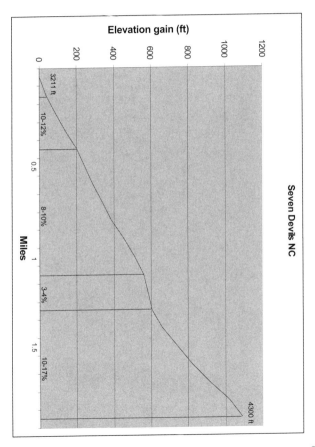

Seven Devils NC

Elevation gain (ft)

3211 ft

10-12%

8-10%

3-4%

10-17%

4300 ft

Miles

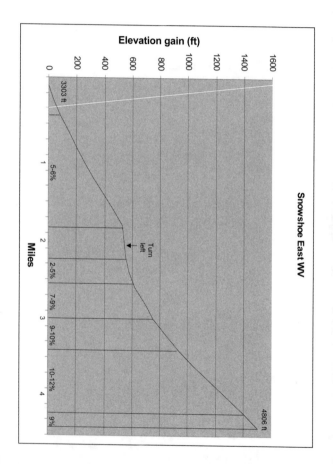

Snowshoe East WV

Elevation gain (ft)

Miles

3303 ft

5-6%

2-5%

7-9%

9-10%

10-12%

9%

4806 ft

Turn left

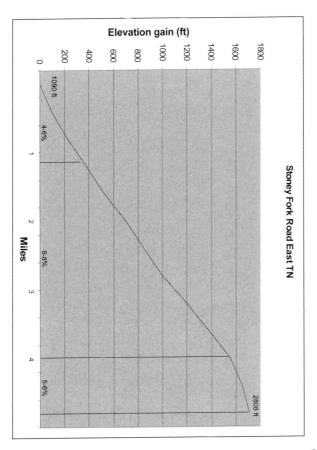

Stoney Fork Road East TN

Elevation gain (ft)

1090 ft

4-6%

Miles

6-8%

5-6%

2808 ft

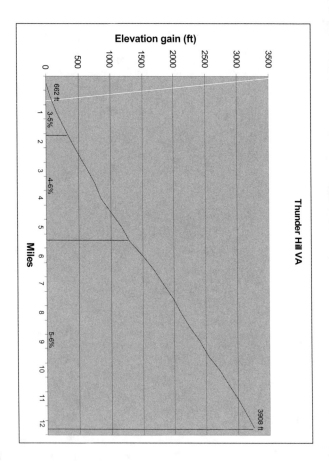

Thunder Hill VA

Elevation gain (ft)

Miles

662 ft

3-5%

4-6%

5-6%

3908 ft

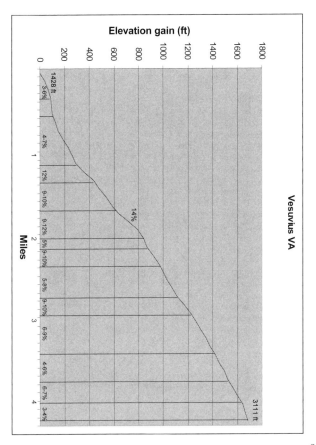

Vesuvius VA

Elevation gain (ft)

Miles

1428 ft
3-6%
4-7%
12%
9-10%
9-12%
14%
5%
9-10%
5-8%
9-10%
6-9%
4-6%
6-7%
3-4%
3111 ft

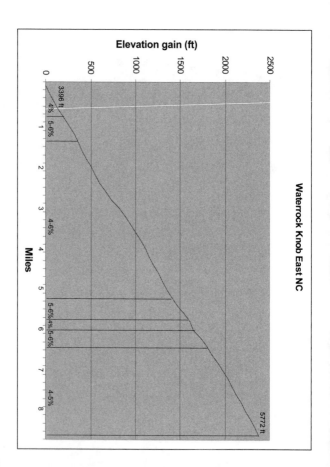

Waterrock Knob East NC

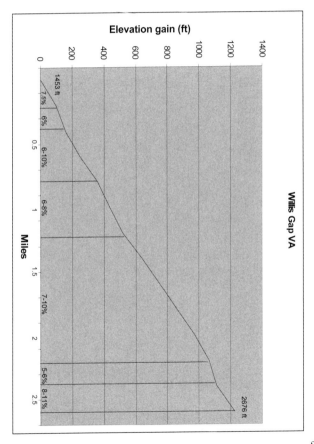

Willis Gap VA

Elevation gain (ft)

Miles

1453 ft

7.5%

6%

6-10%

6-8%

7-10%

5-6% 8-11%

2676 ft

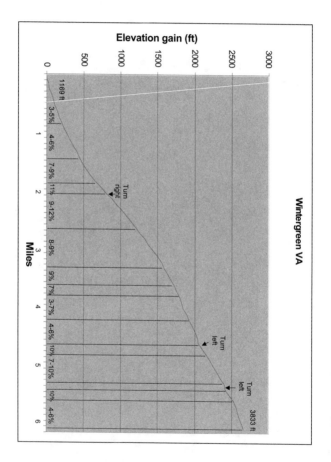

Wintergreen VA

Elevation gain (ft)

1169 ft
3-5%
4-6%
7-9%
11%
Turn right
9-12%
8-9%
9%
7%
3-7%
4-6%
Turn left
10%
7-10%
Turn left
10%
4-6%
3833 ft

Miles

Index

A steep switchback on Virginia's High Knob